A Woman Who Hurts, A God Who Heals

Discovering God's Unconditional Love

By Elsa Kok

New Hope Publishers
Birmingham, Alabama

New Hope Publishers
P. O. Box 12065
Birmingham, AL 35202-2065
www.newhopepubl.com

Library of Congress Cataloging-in-Publication Data

Kok, Elsa, 1968-
  A woman who hurts, a God who heals : discovering unconditional love /
by Elsa Kok.
      p. cm.
ISBN 1-56309-708-7
1. Christian women--Religious life. I. Title.
BV4527 .K65 2002
248.8'43--dc21
2001007002

Cover design by Cheryl Totty
Cover illustration by Cathy Lollar

ISBN: 1-56309-708-7

N024115 • 0502 • 5M1

This book is dedicated to my daughter
Samantha Kelly Lynch
What a treasure you are!
May you continue to build your identity on
and always find your hope in
the deep passionate love of Jesus Christ

Table of Contents

Acknowledgements

To Jesus Christ—You have changed my world in unfathomable ways. I am beyond grateful for your love, I am smitten by your romantic nature, captured by your creativity and head over heals in love with your character. Thank you for giving me the opportunity to shine a light on the passion You have for the broken.

And thank you to the people who have loved me to this place:

◆ *Jennifer Briner*—for reading, editing, loving, encouraging and most of all, for being my Jonathan (and to Eric, for sharing your wife with me!).

◆ *Mom*—for your friendship, your counsel and your prayers. You're such a beautiful, incredible woman of God.

◆ *Dad*—for believing in me and always telling it to me straight.

◆ *Oma and Opa Kok, Oma and Opa VanWaardenberg*—for the legacy of courage, strength and honor that you left to me

◆ *Pieter VanWaarde*—for pastoring our church with such authenticity . . . and for being a great big brother.

◆ *Carol VanWaarde*—for teas, for friendship, for love, for comfort.

◆ *Enno Kok*—for being such a good uncle and a sweet brother. I love you!

◆ *Rob and Laura, John and Wendy (the Koke's)*—for being such wonderful family! You have graciously supported me in so many ways.

◆ *Sherry DeGeorge*—I don't know if you'll ever understand how much your love made a difference in my life.

◆ *Elizabeth Ford*—for grabbing hold of the dream with me, that we may love them to His heart!

◆ *Gretchen Anderson*—You wore the dunces cap with me and we muddled through together. I love you!

◆ *New Hope*—Leslie, Lynn, Trudy, Tara, Shannon, Becky, Rebecca—for all the work you have done on my behalf. What a pleasure it has been to work with you!

- *Esther Kuhns*—for loving me when I was all broken inside.
- *Jerry Jones*—You started all this Jerry. Your friendship literally changed my world. Thank you.
- *Denise Gray*—for bringing me closer to our Savior. We walked through messes together.
- *Thom Bolden*—for always being there when I need you. You are an amazing friend.
- *Ray Scott*—for dinners, for believing in me, for being such an encourager (and for sponsoring my website!).
- *Jeff and Sandy Belden*—I needed you and the chasm was deep. Thank you for being a bridge to Christ.
- *Sue Callamari*—You've loved me since I was twelve. How do I thank you for that?
- *Donna Gates*—for your nurturing care. What a classy woman you are. Your love soothes me.
- *Women of WEB site*—You have walked with me through this. It's been an absolute pleasure and a tremendous growth experience to co-labor with you. I love you!
- *The kids*—Sammy, Piet, Mallory, Curran, Luke, Caleb, Danielle, Rebecca, Ben, Mary, Andrew, James, Nathan, Rachel, Emma—you add tremendous light and joy to my life.
- *Reeses*—for being the best dog around and keeping my feet warm as I write.

$\mathcal{I}$ntroduction

Fellow traveler,

I wish I could sit with you through this study. I wish we could get together once a week over a cup of coffee and see each other face to face. I would look you in the eyes and make sure you know that we are in this together. It's not my desire to tell you everything you should and should not do. I don't want to fill you with fluffy concepts that do nothing to help you in the real-life struggles you are facing. If we could sit with that cup of coffee, I would tell you the real story, the story of my life and the lives of other people I have come to know. This journey is real. God changes everything. When we take the time to really get to know Him, to bring Him all our broken pieces, He changes us in ways beyond what we can imagine.

How do I explain the way I wake up in the morning since I discovered God's unconditional love?

My life has a sense of purpose and joy that it didn't have before. Don't get me wrong—I still have my grumpy days, but my whole perspective on life has changed. It is amazing! Friend, if I could give you any gift in the world, it would be the realization that God is passionately, intensely, and hopelessly in love with you. He wants you as His own. He wants to walk you through every hardship you are facing. He wants to be your rock and your refuge. He wants you to call His name before you reach for anything else, so that He can rescue you, protect you, comfort you, and give you a future.

I know that I can't be with you physically as you walk through this study, but if at all possible, don't do it alone. Find a friend in the church, a mentor, or a group to study with. It is important to have someone who will speak the truth into your life, who will remind you, face to face, how beautiful you are to God. Words in a study are great, but you need the reinforcement of people who love you and love God. Participate. Talk about your feelings; share from your heart. Don't let the enemy rob you of the joy that God is waiting to give you. Too much is at stake. Give this your all.

You'll need one other thing in this process: a journal. Having a journal gives you the opportunity to write your heart. It gives you a recorded history, so you can look back and see how God has worked in your life, and it gives you a place to let loose. Everybody needs a place to go with the hurt and joy of real life. You will be asked to journal three days a week through the study. Hopefully, it will get you in the habit of writing your thoughts and encourage you to continue the practice long after you finish the study.

My prayers are with you. I pray that God will touch your heart through these stories and through His word. I pray that you will be open to receive His love and tenderness. I pray that you will see God in a new way, as your champion and your Savior. I pray as one who has walked a lot of paths that led the wrong way and experienced a lot of the pain that you may now know. I pray as one who longs for you to know a bright hope and a future full of possibility. Seek and you will find. I promise. Better yet, He promises. And that is Truth you can count on.

Elsa Kok

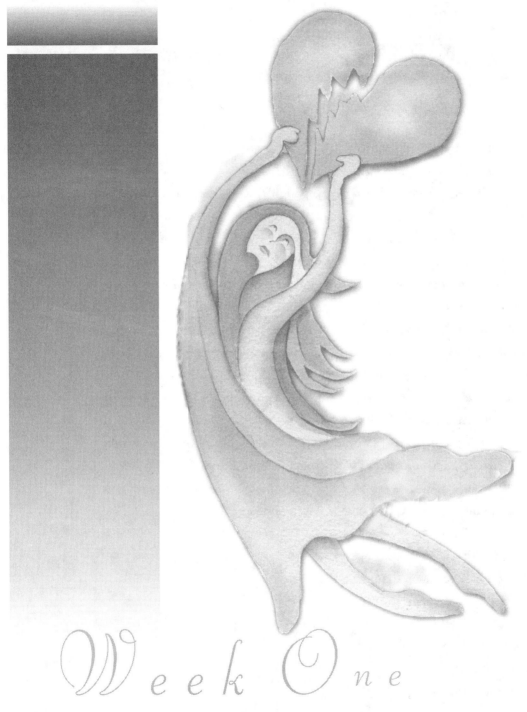

Week One

A Woman Who Hurts, A God Who Heals

Love for Free

Jennifer was thirteen when she first learned to pretend. It started when she had to go to her father's house on the other side of town. Every other weekend she put on the act. She smiled and nodded and acted as if having to live in two separate houses was wonderful. Her parents didn't want to know how she really felt about the divorce. If they did, they would have asked. But they didn't ask. They just smiled and packed her clothes and sent her to each other as if they were exchanging a book or a cup of sugar.

It went fine as long as Jennifer smiled. When her parents saw the anger that boiled inside Jennifer, they blamed each other in heated conversations. When they saw Jennifer's tears, they went into a panic. And when she had trouble at school, or when she left her room a mess, she froze under their silence and disapproval. So Jennifer quickly learned that as long as she didn't get in the way of her parents' happiness, as long as she didn't make them too uncomfortable with what lived inside her, her world moved along just fine.

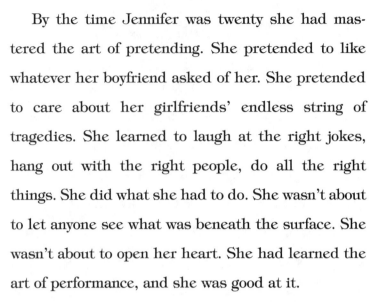

By the time Jennifer was twenty she had mastered the art of pretending. She pretended to like whatever her boyfriend asked of her. She pretended to care about her girlfriends' endless string of tragedies. She learned to laugh at the right jokes, hang out with the right people, do all the right things. She did what she had to do. She wasn't about to let anyone see what was beneath the surface. She wasn't about to open her heart. She had learned the art of performance, and she was good at it.

At twenty-five, Jennifer could feel the bitterness eating away at her. Other people seemed free to do what they wanted, but she couldn't seem to break free. She didn't even know who she was. Someone had told her of a God who loved her just as she was. Jennifer couldn't begin to understand that. No one had ever loved her as she was. There had to be some catch, something she had to do. Love was never free. Even if it was, it certainly wasn't free for her.

A Woman Who Hurts, A God Who Heals

What do you think?

Have you ever had to "act" to be loved? Write a memory that comes to mind.

_____

_____

_____

_____

_____

_____

Do you think you have to be someone different for God to love you—that you have to pretend? How do you think God sees you?

_____

_____

_____

_____

_____

_____

_____

Let's read the Bible . . .

As Jesus and his disciples were on their way, he came to a village where a woman named Martha opened her home to him. She had a sister called Mary, who sat at the Lord's feet listening to what he said. But Martha was distracted by all the preparations that had to be made. She came to him and asked, "Lord, don't you care that my sister has left me to do the work by myself? Tell her to help me!"

"Martha, Martha," the Lord answered, "you are worried and upset about many things, but only one thing is needed. Mary has chosen what is better, and it will not be taken away from her."
—Luke 10:38–42

What do these verses mean for us?

In this story, Jesus visits Mary and Martha. You can imagine that they wanted the house to be clean and the meal perfect. It was all Martha could think about. Things had to be perfect for everyone there. Mary, on the other hand, just wanted to hear what Jesus had to say. So what if there were a couple of dirty dishes? Who cares if they had to eat leftovers? She knew Jesus loved her, not her house, her skills

A Woman Who Hurts, A God Who Heals

as a hostess, or her ability to jump through all the right hoops. His love was for her, pure and simple.

Martha was angry. She wanted Mary to help clean and prepare. Maybe she thought that Jesus would be displeased if everything wasn't perfect. Maybe someone had taught Martha that she wouldn't know love unless she performed just right.

So what can we take from these verses? We don't have to pretend with God. He has no hoops for us to jump through, no checklists, no "perfect life" requirements. All He wants from us is—us. He wants to sit with us and love us. He aches to share His heart with us. In fact, He wants that more than He wants perfection or pretense. When He said to Martha, "Mary has chosen what is better," He said the same to us. If we choose to simply sit and be, He will share with us His story and His love.

How can we apply these verses?

When you get ready to do this Bible study, imagine sitting at the feet of Jesus as He tells you about who He really is. How do you think it would feel to sit and listen to Him in person?

_____

_____

_____

_____

_____

Do you want to ask Him to show you something in particular? Write a little prayer from your heart. Is it hard to believe that you don't have to "clean up" or act differently to receive His love? Do you believe He loves you no matter what? Write whatever you're feeling. He wants this time with you!

_____

_____

_____

_____

A Woman Who Hurts, A God Who Heals

Your love letter . . .

When you receive Jesus into your heart, you become adopted into the family of God. You become His daughter—for always. The Bible is His love letter to you. It may seem hard to believe—God writing a love letter to you? It's true! His heart is full of love for you. Of course, letting that sink from your head to your heart might take some time. That's okay. He will walk every step with you. He will help you understand how big and full and true His love is. It's a gift; it's not earned. You don't have to act, pretend, or become someone else . . . He loves you just as you are.

Every week we will take a verse and create a love letter. The letter will be from God to you. This week, I will do it for you. Simply put your name in the blank, and take the words as yours. These are God's thoughts to you. Take them into your heart and savor them. He loves you so much!

> "For it is by grace you have been saved, through faith—and this not from yourselves, it is the gift of God—not by works, so that no one can boast. For we are God's workmanship" (Ephesians 2:8–10a).

Dear _____,

You have been saved by grace, because you believe in Me. This didn't happen because of anything you did. If My love were based on all the stuff you do, then people would compare themselves to each other. Some would think they were better than others. I wanted to avoid that. I wanted you to know that this is My gift to you, My work-manship and My pride and joy. I designed you! I put My heart into creating you. You are Mine.

    I love you

    God

More verses . . .

Still don't believe He loves you just as you are? Check out these verses for more love letters to you.

Romans 8:37

Psalm 146:7–9

1 John 3:1

Psalm 139:1–16

Psalm 145:8–9, 13b–14,17–18

John 3:16

Journal time . . .

Journal at least three days this week. Read the verses listed above, and pick three that you can apply to your life right now. On each day you journal, write the verse you chose and what it means for you. You can make it into a love letter or just write how it applies to you. Ask God to help you understand what He is saying to you.

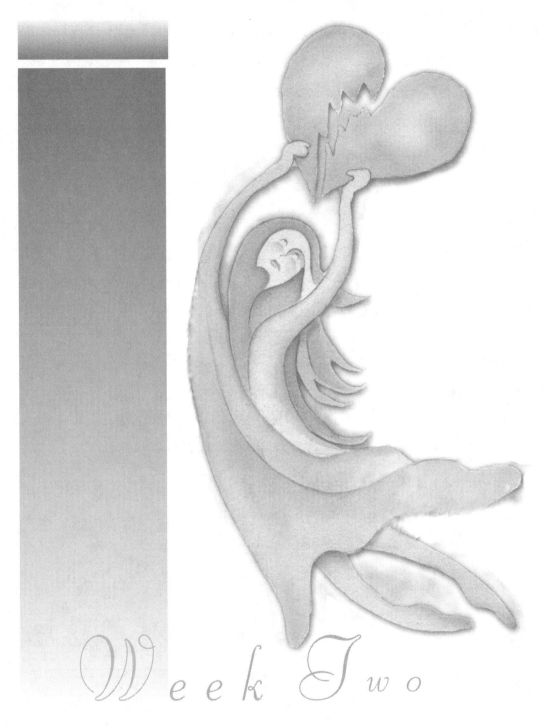

Week Two

A Woman Who Hurts, A God Who Heals

There Is Hope

Anna stumbled. Her heart was racing. She picked up the edges of her dress and ran faster. She tripped over a tree root and almost went sprawling. But she didn't care. She had to get back and tell them what had happened. At the edge of town, she stopped to catch her breath.

Anna sat on a rock and breathed deeply. The man at the well had known her, really known her! She thought of His kind face, His loving and gentle eyes. She had never seen eyes like that. The man's name was Jesus, and in a moment, He'd become life to her. Every man Anna had ever known treated her like the dirt now spattered on her dress. She'd been yelled at, cursed at, and abused. But never had anyone talked to her as Jesus did. Never had anyone seen into her heart so clearly.

He knew everything about her. He knew that she had been with five husbands. Each of them turned her away. He knew that she was now living with someone else who wouldn't think of marrying her. His eyes told her that He knew of the endless nights that she spent in tears, the heart-wrenching feeling of being used, of being completely deserted. He offered her something different—a hope and a future.

Anna pinched herself. It truly seemed like an impossible dream. Why did He talk to her? She was, after all, a woman. Men didn't talk to women, especially with kindness. They definitely didn't speak to someone like her, someone with a past. She was also a Samaritan, and He was a Jew. Jews didn't mingle with Samaritans. It was unheard of!

Then she thought of His goodness. She had seen it in His eyes. He was pure. She knew of a hundred women who hadn't made the same mistakes she had made. She knew of good young girls, faithful wives—people who didn't have so much guilt in their lives. If Jesus was going to talk to someone, why did He choose her?

Living water. He had offered her something called "living water," and her heart leapt at the thought. He promised that if she drank the living water, she would never thirst again. The living water was Jesus; her heart told her so. So if she believed Jesus, could that possibly mean that she wouldn't thirst for a man's touch with such desperation? Did

A Woman Who Hurts, A God Who Heals

it mean that she might one day walk without the longings and the hurts and the aches? Did it mean that she could have something better than the lonely, painful life she'd been living?

She dared to hope.

Enjoy the story of Jesus' encounter with a Samaritan woman. You can find it in John 4.

What do you think?

Can you relate to the woman at the well? In what ways can you relate to the loneliness and hurt from her past?

_____

_____

_____

_____

Do you believe that God has a future in mind for you? If not, why?

_____

_____

_____

_____

Take a moment to imagine how it would be if Jesus came to you now—if He took your hand, looked you in the eyes, and offered you more than the life you have known. What if He did that without looking down on you, without judging you? What if He did it because He loves you right where you are and wants you to know freedom from the things that hurt you? Take a moment to imagine, and describe how these things would feel to you.

A Woman Who Hurts, A God Who Heals

Let's read the Bible . . .

"But those who hope in the Lord will renew their strength. They will soar on wings like eagles; they will run and not grow weary, they will walk and not be faint." —Isaiah 40:31

What does this verse mean for us?

For me, when I first thought about a real future, I felt overwhelmed. I couldn't imagine living without the hurt, the pain, the addictions, and the men. I wanted to, but I was scared. I didn't think the God stuff applied to me. Soar on wings like eagles? Run and not grow weary? They were pretty pictures, but what did they have to do with my life?

My fellow traveler, they have everything to do with our lives! Remember the woman at the well? She went back to town and told everyone about Jesus. People's lives were changed because of her. Can you imagine how she felt? After she had known nothing but rejection, she was suddenly the center of attention! She went from the lowest of the low to the one God Himself chose to talk with. I bet she felt eagle-like.

So, we ask, how? How did her future change?

What did she have to do? All she had to do was believe what He was telling her. She had to "hope in the Lord." There must have been something very real in her connection with Jesus at the well. She must have seen something that made it easy for her to believe. Yet, we can't see His eyes, so how do we believe? We ask Him. With whatever words, with whatever feelings come, we need to ask God for help. *God, I don't understand how this works, but I need You. I want to believe You have more for me. Or, God, please help.* I don't want to put words into your mouth, but whatever you want to ask, He will hear, and He will help you. He will also help you believe and hope.

How can we apply it?

Use this space to write a few words to God. What is on your heart? Use this moment to ask for His help.

_____

_____

_____

_____

_____

A Woman Who Hurts, A God Who Heals

Your love letter . . .

Remember, God gave us the Bible to help us understand more about Him. He gave us the words and the stories to show us who He is. We can take His promises literally! Add a line of your own to this love letter. Don't worry about whether it sounds just right; simply study the verses below, and see what God says to your heart.

For this week's love letter, we will use Jeremiah 29:11–13: "'For I know the plans I have for you,' declares the Lord, 'plans to prosper you and not to harm you, plans to give you hope and a future. Then you will call upon me and come and pray to me, and I will listen to you. You will seek me and find me when you seek me with all your heart.'"

Dear _____,

I have plans for you, a future. I want to give you good things and bring hope into your life. _____, I love you. Hope in Me, believe in Me, think about Me, and I will turn the sad, dark places inside your heart into fields of sunshine and hope. I will give you the things you need and bring you close to Me. Call to Me. Talk to Me. I will be there. Like a true friend, I will listen to every word.

_____

_____

_____

_____

_____

_____

_____

Hold on to Me.
   I love you always,
   God

More verses . . .

For other messages of your hope and future, look at these verses:

Hebrews 10:22–23

Psalm 30:11–12

Psalm 68:19–20

John 15:10–11

Matthew 11:28–30

Journal time . . .

Journal at least three days this week. Read the verses listed above, and pick three that you can apply to your life right now. On each day you journal, write the verse you chose and what it means for you. Ask God to help you understand what He is saying to you. Write what His promises mean to your life right now.

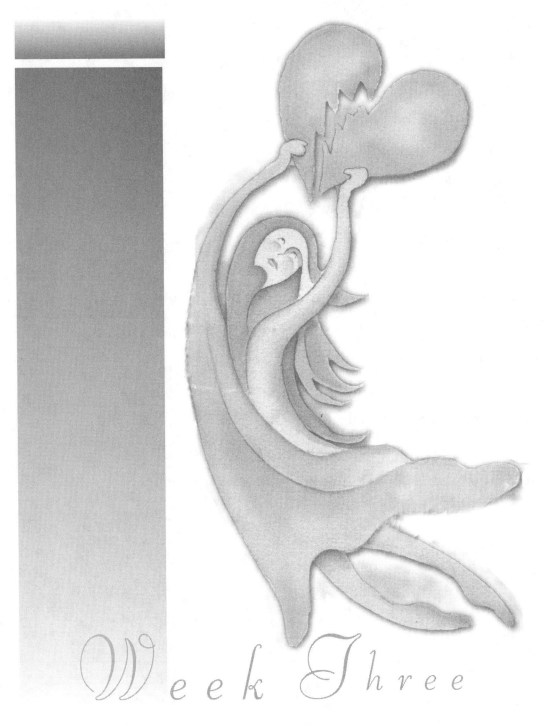

Week Three

A Woman Who Hurts, A God Who Heals

White as Snow

Shannon sat cross-legged on the floor, her head bowed low. Her eyes were closed, and her heart was racing. It was as if someone had just turned on a light, and she could see the dirty, broken pieces inside her heart. She felt guilty, horribly guilty. She had never taken the time to look at her past. In fact, she had conveniently forgotten about her greatest act of betrayal. Stealing a boyfriend was one thing, but stealing a husband was a hundred times worse. Shame flooded her being as she remembered her lies, the way she plotted and maneuvered her way into his arms. There were other things—the times as a teenager she had broken her mother's heart and the time she'd stolen money from her boss.

The previous Sunday, she had listened to the sermon about God's forgiveness and love. She was trying to get her life back on track, but how could she forgive or forget the past? More importantly, how could God forgive or forget? Surely He was furious with her. He might forgive some of her sins, but how could He possibly forgive the others? This was too easy; she felt as if she was copping out to receive a clean slate. Didn't God know the depth of the sin that lived inside her? Hadn't He given up on her long ago?

Shannon rested her face in her hands, the weight of her past heavy upon her. She would give anything to be rid of the pain. She would walk a thousand miles, work a thousand years, and pay all the money she had. That seemed fair. That seemed right.

Could she receive forgiveness with nothing to give in return? Could she accept that Jesus, the Son of God, died 2000 years ago so she could know freedom from her burden of sadness? What if this was really true?

Shannon tried to imagine standing at the foot of the cross. She imagined that she knew the man hanging there, gasping for His last few breaths. She pictured His eyes and the tenderness and love in them. Did this Jesus, who was so willing to free her, see something in her that she hadn't yet discovered? Did a glimmer of hope exist for her?

Something inside Shannon stirred and responded to the tenderness of the vision. Something felt

A Woman Who Hurts, A God Who Heals

true. Shannon knew that if such a story were true, if she could hold on to a love such as that, everything would change. That scared her and excited her all at once.

Could it be true?

What do you think?

Is it hard for you to imagine Jesus dying for you? Do sins or events come to mind that you don't think God would forgive? You don't necessarily have to share these with anyone (though I encourage you to talk with someone you trust), but write a word or two about them.

_____

_____

_____

_____

Do you feel that you can personally experience the forgiveness and love of Jesus? Why or why not?

_____

_____

_____

_____

Let's read the Bible . . .

"'For God so loved the world that he gave his one and only Son, that whoever believes in him shall not perish but have eternal life. For God did not send his Son into the world to condemn the world, but to save the world through him.'"

—John 3:16–17

What do these verses mean for us?

Eternal life is ours, and not only that, it was meant for us. Growing up, I used to believe that God loved only the religious people. I didn't bother to look in the Bible and find the stories that would have told me otherwise. Jesus opens the door for us all. He wants us all. In fact, His heart is especially tender to those of us who have gone through the ringer in one way or another.

Nobody is perfect. Do you find yourself comparing your life to others? Do you think that someone else deserves heaven but you don't? I've thought that, too. Yet, if we read the verses above, we see that God includes each of us in that statement. In fact, you could substitute the word "world" for your name. Try it.

A Woman Who Hurts, A God Who Heals

"For God so loved _____ that he gave his one and only Son, that [if] _____ believes in him _____ shall not perish but have eternal life. For God did not send his Son [to] _____ to condemn _____, but to save _____ through him" (author's paraphrase). Feels good, doesn't it?

We tend to think that God is crossing His arms, tapping His foot, and waiting for us to get it right. Instead, He is opening His arms and longing for us to run into them. He wants to hold us tight and separate us from the sin and the brokenness that have hurt us for so long. No sin is too big for God to forgive! He doesn't say, "For God so loved the world (except those who have committed adultery) that he gave his one and only Son (except to those who have done drugs and stolen from their parents), that whoever believes in him (except those who should have known better) . . ." No, He doesn't say that! He wants us all so that He can dust us off, wipe us clean, and give us new life in Him.

How can we apply them?

Imagine taking those events and sins to the cross, setting them down, and knowing that the price has been paid. Use the following space to write a short prayer. It might look something like this: "Lord, forgive me for . . ." or "Father, I need Your help; this hurts . . ."

_____

_____

_____

_____

_____

_____

_____

_____

_____

_____

_____

_____

_____

Remember, while God completely forgives the sin the moment we call out to Him, it can still hurt. God isn't going anywhere; He'll walk us through as time heals the hurt.

A Woman Who Hurts, A God Who Heals

Your love letter . . .

(We'll combine two Scriptures this week.)

"Therefore, if anyone is in Christ, he is a new creation; the old has gone, the new has come!" (2 Corinthians 5:17).

"If we confess our sins, he is faithful and just and will forgive us our sins and purify us from all unrighteousness" (1 John 1:9).

Dearest _____,

Once you believed in Me and accepted Me into your heart, you became a new creation. It may not always feel new, but that's okay. Sin is going to come into your life, and sometimes you will slip up. Memories will come, and they will hurt. Come to Me; tell Me what you're feeling.

_____, tell Me about the ache in your heart and the sadness that came as you stepped over the line. I'm not here to condemn you; I'm here to teach you how to live in a new and different way that will bring you joy like you've never known. _____

_____

_____

_____

_____

_____

_____

Love,

God

More verses . . .

Psalm 103:2–5

Matthew 1:21

Romans 5:6–8

Psalm 40:1–3

Romans 8:1–2

Psalm 30:11–12

Journal time . . .

Look at these verses as though they were love letters left on your pillow. What is your Savior saying to you this week? Write your thoughts in your journal on three different days.

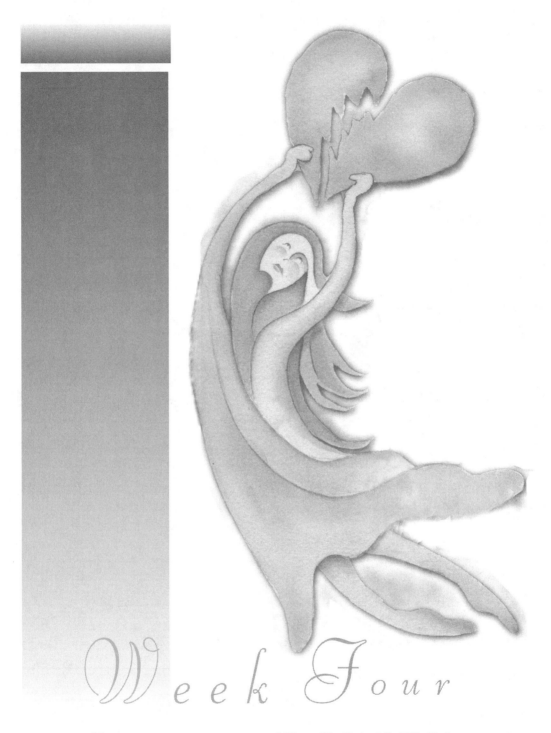

Week Four

A Woman Who Hurts, A God Who Heals

It's Okay to Cry

Micah lay in bed, curled up on her side. She imagined a shattered picture frame on the floor. Underneath the broken pieces of glass lay a photo of what should have been. All her life she'd dreamed of her own family—she was going to love being a wife and a mother. When she was a child, she imagined what true love looked like. She knew it would be beautiful—that it would sweep her away and that she'd live happily ever after. She also knew that one day she would be successful—as strong in her career as she was in her home life. She would have it all.

But then life happened. Everything she had dreamed of was stripped away. She had no true love, no successful career—just life, with addictions and needs and pains that consumed her.

A tear spilled onto her cheek, and she wiped it away fiercely. What was the point of crying now? There was no going back, no changing the past. She simply had to accept that life had thrown her a curve ball, and she never saw it coming.

Another tear escaped. What was wrong with her?

Why did it hurt so badly? Surely the future would be better; surely things would work out in the end. So everything hadn't turned out exactly as—or even remotely near—what she had hoped. Micah felt the sob come up from the depth of her belly. She couldn't help it. It did hurt—so much that she could hardly breathe from the weight of it. She wanted the life she dreamed of as a child. She wanted the loving husband, the smart children, the budding career. She hated the hopelessness that seemed to eat at her, and she despised the voice inside that said she had lost it all forever.

Micah felt ashamed. Crying seemed such a waste of time. She was having a pity party, but she couldn't help it. Losing her childhood dream felt a little like death, like the loss of someone very close, and she grieved for it.

So Micah cried.

What do you think?

Have you ever felt the sadness of a broken dream?
Write a paragraph about it.

_____

_____

_____

_____

_____

_____

_____

Do you believe that God sees and cares about your
tears? Has there been a time when you've felt God's
presence alongside you as you cried?

_____

_____

_____

_____

_____

_____

_____

_____

Let's read the Bible . . .

"He was despised and rejected by men, a man of sorrows, and familiar with suffering . . . Surely he took up our infirmities and carried our sorrows."
—Isaiah 53:3–4a

What do these verses mean for us?

If anyone can understand the heartbreak of lost dreams, Jesus can. He came to earth and was completely rejected by the very people He had come to save. They despised Him! They made fun of Him. His life was filled with pain and loss. When He came to the end of His life and went into the garden of Gethsemane to pray, He said, "My soul is overwhelmed with sorrow to the point of death" (Mark 14:34).

Jesus knew that He would be asked to give up His life as a sacrifice for us. What a difficult thing! How did He respond? He didn't say, "This is what my life is about; I just have to deal with it" or "What's the point of crying? It's not going to change anything." Jesus knew something that we sometimes forget: The Father, God Himself, cares about our tears. He wants us to come to Him with our sadness. He weeps with us and holds us. It doesn't matter whether our choices or our circumstances cause our loss; it's still a loss. The tears are the same, and the Father cares.

There is something incredibly moving about a broken heart. When we act tough and pretend that we're okay, we lose the opportunity to share a precious moment with God. Each of us deals with broken dreams. Each of us has loss. Much of my loss came from my own terrible choices. I made mistakes, and those mistakes cost me a lot. It wasn't until I came to God and cried out my heart for what might have been that I felt a change in our relationship. Suddenly, He wasn't some distant being who didn't care; He was someone who cried with me.

How can we apply them?

Knowing that Jesus dealt with great sorrow, knowing that all of us live with sadness over things that might have been, would you be willing to come to Jesus with your broken dreams? Take a moment and imagine that He is sitting beside you, holding your hand. He lifts your chin with His other hand and looks you in the eyes. "Tell Me about the sadness I see," He says. What would you say to our Lord?

_____

_____

_____

_____

_____

_____

_____

_____

_____

_____

A Woman Who Hurts, A God Who Heals

Your love letter . . .

God promises that we are not alone. When we deal with the heartache and heartbreak in our lives, He comforts us. Sometimes we run to other things: we eat too much, we drink too much, we hide. But only Jesus has the healing touch, the tender heart, the compassionate eyes.

The following verses are a portion of God's promise. This time I will only write a few of the lines. You fill in the rest. Let God touch your heart as you write the letter. These words are for you!

"Fear not, for I have redeemed you; I have summoned you by name; you are mine. When you pass through the waters, I will be with you; and when you pass through the rivers, they will not sweep over you. When you walk through the fire, you will not be burned; the flames will not set you ablaze. For I am the Lord, your God, the Holy One of Israel, your Savior. . . . Since you are precious and honored in My sight, and because I love you . . ." —Isaiah 43:1–4.

Dearest _____,

Don't be scared, My dear one. You are Mine. When life seems overwhelming, when it feels as if you are drowning in your sadness, I will be there. The raging river of your pain will not drag you under if you cling to Me.

_____

_____

_____

_____

_____

_____

_____

_____

_____

_____

_____

I love you,

God

More verses . . .

Matthew 11:28

2 Corinthians 1:3–4

Psalm 62:8

Psalm 30:11–12

Isaiah 40:1–2

Psalm 23

Journal time . . .

Journal at least three days this week. Read the verses listed above, and pick three that you can apply to your life right now. On each day you journal, write the verse you chose and what it means for you. Ask God to help you understand what He is saying to you.

Let God share His heart of comfort with you.

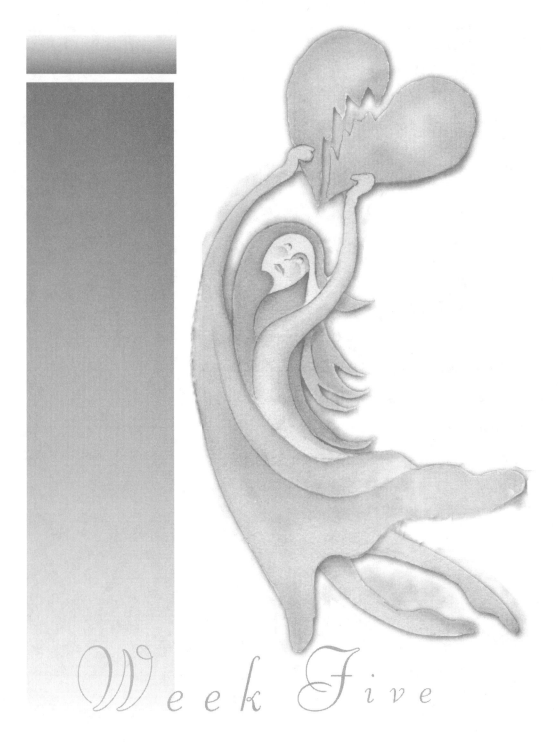

Week Five

A Woman Who Hurts, A God Who Heals

Frustrated Ever After

Elizabeth stared at the door and felt the loneliness creep in with the quiet. John would not be coming over that night. Their relationship was over—for good. Elizabeth felt the tightness in her chest, the longing in her belly. She didn't want to be alone; she hated the sound of her breathing against the backdrop of silence. Even when she turned on the TV, the noise did nothing to drown out the cries of her heart.

She didn't know what went wrong. When she met John she felt the butterflies, the hope, the breathtaking excitement. She wasn't innocent enough to think that everything would be perfect, but she hadn't expected it to end so swiftly—again.

All her life, Elizabeth knew she would one day meet him—the man who was meant for her, who would fill the hole in her heart and make it okay. She was starting to lose hope. No one seemed right. She wondered whether something was wrong with her—whether she was so broken inside that no one could love her. Or maybe, she thought in quiet desperation, I've just picked the wrong guys, and the right one is still waiting out there.

Elizabeth never admitted her thoughts to anyone. Her friends would laugh if they knew how much her heart longed to be swept away and romanced. She was tough on the outside, but inside, her childhood dreams lingered. She wanted the "happily ever after"—the Cinderella story. But she was starting to lose hope.

The fairy tale story, with the knight who would sweep her off her feet, was turning into a cruel hoax. Elizabeth sighed, deeply saddened. Could no one fix the holes? Could no relationship bring her the joy and security she longed for?

Terrified, Elizabeth shivered. If no one could fix the holes, who was going to make her okay?

A Woman Who Hurts, A God Who Heals

What do you think?

Can you identify with the story above? Have you ever felt that meeting the right guy would make everything else in your life come together? Describe what you hope for in a relationship (whether a current relationship or a future one).

_____

_____

_____

_____

_____

There is nothing wrong with longing for a relationship. Only when we think that a relationship will fix us do we end up feeling completely let down. Have you ever been disappointed by a relationship or a person who didn't fill the ache in your heart? Describe that situation.

_____

_____

_____

_____

_____

Remember the Samaritan woman whose story we heard in Chapter Two? Here was a woman who had been married five times and was now living with a guy. Talk about being let down! Her dreams for a happily ever after had been completely shattered long before she met Jesus. He offered her something more, something that would ease the ache and fill her as no man could.

Let's read the Bible . . .

"'But whoever drinks the water I give him will never thirst. Indeed, the water I give him will become in him a spring of water welling up to eternal life.' The woman said to him, 'Sir, give me this water so that I won't get thirsty.'"
—John 4:14–15

What do these verses mean for us?

Through the story of the Samaritan woman, Jesus tells us that He is the source of our joy. He told her that if she continued to go to the same places to satisfy her thirst, she would keep coming up empty. She would get thirsty again. I know that feeling. Don't you? I used to believe that as long as I had

A Woman Who Hurts, A God Who Heals

someone in my life, everything else would fall into place. I believed that if I found the right guy, I would be happy, so I kept looking. Relationships weren't designed to be our everything; they fall apart if we think they should be. No one can be our *everything*— no one except Jesus. Jesus promises that when we depend on Him, when we are in close relationship to Him, we can depend on Him for comfort and joy and He will be there.

So how does it work? It sounds simple and nice and religious, but how do we get this living water He talks about? I'll tell you what I've discovered. My happily ever after is totally dependent on my relationship with Jesus. I am still learning how to connect to the Living Water. Some days I call out to Him in my loneliness and find that two hours later I feel peaceful and comforted. I won't know how it happened, and sometimes (though I'm ashamed to admit it) I'm surprised He has answered me. But He does answer me, sometimes through my friendships, sometimes through a sermon, sometimes through this quiet contentment that takes over in my heart.

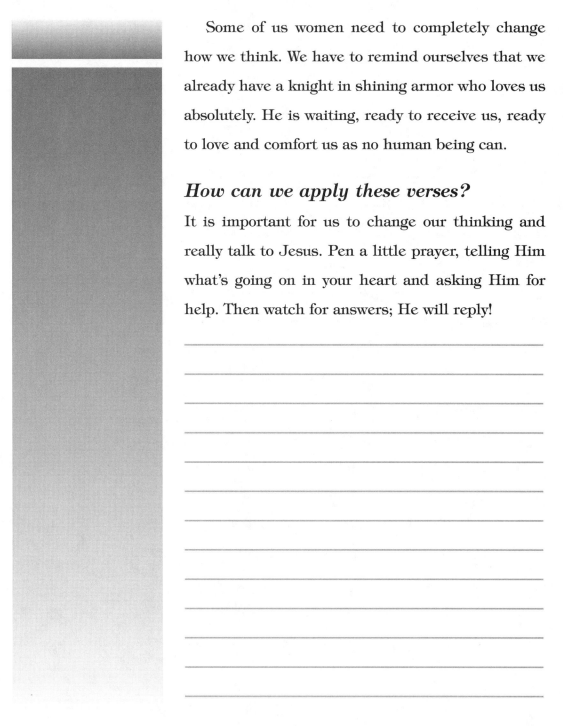

Some of us women need to completely change how we think. We have to remind ourselves that we already have a knight in shining armor who loves us absolutely. He is waiting, ready to receive us, ready to love and comfort us as no human being can.

How can we apply these verses?

It is important for us to change our thinking and really talk to Jesus. Pen a little prayer, telling Him what's going on in your heart and asking Him for help. Then watch for answers; He will reply!

Your love letter . . .

Because this Scripture has a lot of symbolism, I will help with this letter. I am interpreting what I believe God is saying to us, based on the knowledge of His character and the evidence of His heart throughout Scripture.

> "'Come, all you who are thirsty, come to the waters; and you who have no money, come, buy and eat! Come, buy wine and milk without money and without cost. Why spend money on what is not bread, and your labor on what does not satisfy? Listen, listen to me, and eat what is good, and your soul will delight in the richest of fare. Give ear and come to me; hear me, that your soul may live.'" —Isaiah 55:1–3

Dearest _____,

Come to Me, My sweet _____.
Come to the one place where your heart can be
filled. There is no cost, nothing you have to pay.
My love is free, and it is yours. When you expect
someone else to do My job, you will be disappointed. You will give yourself away and receive nothing
in return. Don't give your heart away to receive
what only I can give.

Come to Me, talk to Me, lean on Me. I will fill
you to the brim with My love and My hope. Then
your heart will shine brightly and overflow into your
other relationships. You will be full of good food,
so that you will love out of your fullness, not out
of your emptiness. How rich that will make your
relationships, your soul, your life!

Hold on to Me, walk with Me, and listen to
these words. I have so much for you!

With tremendous love,
Jesus

More verses . . .

John 7:37–38

Psalm 91:14–15

Psalm 107: 8–9

Psalm 33:18–22

Psalm 81:10

John 6:35

Journal time . . .

More love letters await you in the verses above.
Journal at least three days this week.

Read them, write them in your journal, and apply
them to your life. They are for you!

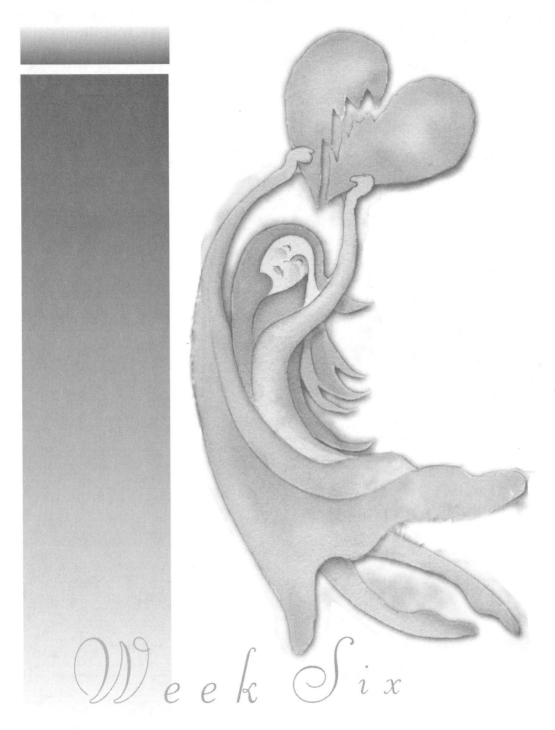

Week Six

A Woman Who Hurts, A God Who Heals

The Truth

Sarah stood before the crowd of men. Her head was bowed, her eyes squeezed tightly shut. The men were going to stone her, and she deserved it. She'd been caught as an adulteress. She wished that at least he loved her; then perhaps the punishment would feel nobler. But Sarah knew better. There was no love in his arms. She felt used and broken—familiar feelings. She knew that she was only worth what her body could offer.

She hoped that she would die quickly.

The crowd shoved Sarah in front of Jesus. They said, "Teacher, this woman was caught in the act of adultery. In the Law, Moses commanded us to stone such women. Now what do you say?" Silence. Sarah held her breath as she imagined the first stone flying through the air and cutting her skin.

The men badgered Jesus for an answer. Sarah braved a glance at Him. He was kneeling in the dirt, drawing something in the sand. Sarah watched the men around Him strain to see what He had written.

Finally, He spoke, and He looked at Sarah with great tenderness and compassion. "If any one of you is without sin," He said softly, turning His eyes to the crowd, "let him be the first to throw a stone at her." He lowered His eyes to the ground.

Sarah waited for the first stone while Jesus wrote in the sand again. Incredibly, people started to walk away. Some went quickly, furtively. Others went reluctantly, looking back at her with barely contained regret.

Then only Sarah and Jesus remained. "Where are they? Has no one condemned you?" He asked.

Sarah shook her head. "No one, sir." Her heart flooded with relief, disbelief, and joy.

"Then neither do I condemn you," He said. His look of love spoke volumes to her heart. The man who used her for her body had quickly abandoned her. Now this teacher, Jesus, who should have led the stoning, looked at her with love. Why did He care about her? She could see that He did, that He loved her. She could see that to Him, she was valuable. Why else would He face an angry crowd and save her life? Her mind was racing. "Go now," He said with the same tenderness, "and leave your life of sin."

Sarah continued to look at Him in disbelief. Even His final words, to leave her sin, were said with an urgent, protective tone, as though He cared about her, about the state of her heart, and about her choices—as though He had a stake in her life and wanted more for her. *As though I am important to Him, she thought.*

Read John 8 for the full story.

What do you think?

Sarah was valuable and precious to Jesus. When she committed adultery, perhaps she crossed the line to please a man and maybe even to feel a kind of love. Yet Jesus loved her simply because of who she was. She was important to Him. Have you ever crossed a line for someone because you wanted to feel close to him, though you knew it wasn't about love? Describe that time.

_____

_____

_____

_____

_____

_____

If you stood in front of a crowd as Sarah did, what do you believe Jesus would do? Why?

_____

_____

_____

_____

_____

A Woman Who Hurts, A God Who Heals

Let's read the Bible . . .

"Where can I go from your Spirit? Where can I flee from your presence? If I go up to the heavens, you are there; if I make my bed in the depths, you are there. If I rise on the wings of the dawn, if I settle on the far side of the sea, even there your hand will guide me, your right hand will hold me fast. . . . For you created my inmost being; you knit me together in my mother's womb. I praise you because I am fearfully and wonderfully made; your works are wonderful, I know that full well."

—Psalm 139:7–10,13–14

What do these verses mean for us?

These verses means everything to us! They means that long ago, when we were inside our mother's womb, God had His hand on us. He gave us a certain smile, the color of our eyes, the gifts of our hands. He gave us a singing voice or a tender heart, a gift for creativity or a sharp mind. He loves us because He handcrafted us from the beginning, and He loves us no matter where we are in life!

It took me a while to truly believe that I was valuable and precious to God. I kept trying to get other people to tell me that. It didn't matter whether those people cared about my best interests. As long as they told me or seemed to believe that I was special, I wanted them in my life. Even in my relationships with men, even when it was bad, I often stayed for those rare moments that I felt loved.

That's the key: Jesus loves us—completely and perfectly. He loves us through the hurts and through the joys. It is impossible for Him *not* to love us. How could He turn away from someone He designed? Whether we are closely connected to Him or living far from His ways, His heart is full of love for us. He wants us home, close and warm and safe and far from the depths that destroy us.

How can we apply these verses?

I want you to think for a moment about how precious you are. Write five things about you that God designed. As you write them, remember that His love and His pride in us make us valuable, because we are His.

A Woman Who Hurts, A God Who Heals

When we look into the mirror, we often quickly find fault. See if you can look into the mirror without finding all the imperfections. What color are your eyes? Do you have laugh lines? Dimples? You are a miracle! Do you know that? A handcrafted, perfectly designed, glorious miracle of God. You may not feel that way right now, and it may be hard to hold your own gaze, but you will in time. Jesus can't live in your heart without reminding you that you are His and that you are a treasure!

Your love letter . . .

"Israel, whom I have chosen. This is what the Lord says—he who made you, who formed you in the womb, and who will help you: Do not be afraid, O Jacob, my servant, Jeshurun, whom I have chosen. For I will pour water on the thirsty land, and streams on the dry ground." —Isaiah 44:1–3

Dearest _____, whom I have chosen,
This is what I say, the One who created you,
_____. Listen to Me, for I made
you even as you lay inside your mother's belly. Don't
ever be afraid, sweet _____, for I
will help you. You are precious to Me! All of the life
stuff—the frustrations, the sadness, the pain—can be
like dry, barren places in your heart. I will refresh
those places; I will help you. When you feel alone or
unloved, I will comfort you. With that one worry
(write it here) _____

_____

_____

_____

_____

_____

I will be here; you are not alone.
        I love you!
        God

More verses . . .

Jeremiah 31:3–4

Isaiah 43:1–4

Psalm 145:17–20

Zephaniah 3:17

1 John 3:1

Isaiah 30:18

Journal time . . .

Let God use these verses to remind you how valuable you are to Him. Journal at least three days this week. Read the verses listed above, and pick three that you can apply to your life right now. On each day you journal, write the verse you chose and what it means for you. Ask God to help you understand what He is saying to you.

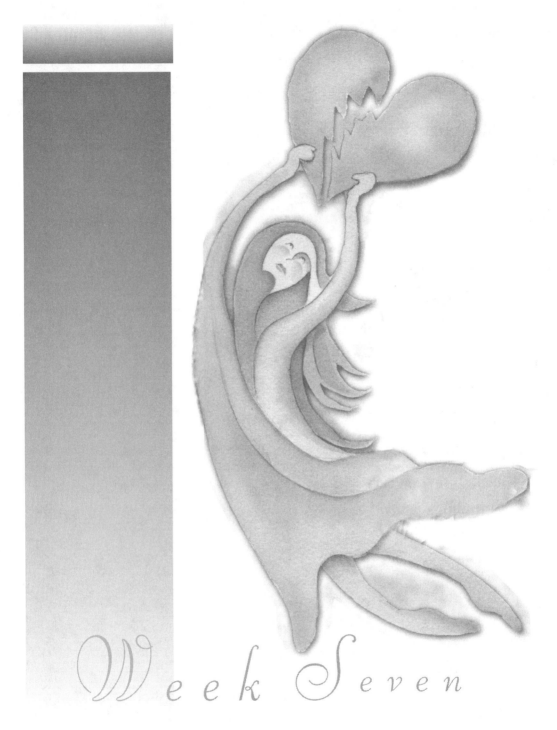

Week Seven

A Woman Who Hurts, A God Who Heals

*Y*our Pearls

Laura couldn't imagine giving up sex. Somewhere inside she thought it might be a good idea, but it was hard to imagine trying to be pure after the life she had led. Not only that, but she wasn't sure what a romantic relationship without sex was like. She'd never been in one. How do people connect without sex? Do they just hold hands? How silly is that? Laura couldn't imagine it.

Besides, it seemed so old-fashioned. She hardly knew anyone who waited until marriage anymore. What's the big deal?

Laura knew that the Bible taught something different. She knew that it talked about sex and the importance of staying pure. But did that really apply to her? It was written so long ago; what could the Bible say about today's world?

Laura sighed. Part of her wished she had waited. She couldn't imagine making love for the first time on her wedding night. How beautiful that might have been! But the chance of that was long gone. Was it possible to change now? Could she promise to stay pure until God brought her the right man and they married?

Something in Laura responded to that dream. Was it truly too late for her to be pure? Could someone love her without sex? Could she love someone without it? If they didn't hide in sex, would the relationship have any substance?

Laura closed her eyes. A strange longing filled her heart. For the first time in her life she wondered if there was more to sex than what she'd imagined. After all, there had to be a reason for her sadness, the regret she felt the morning after. If it was all fine and dandy, if it wasn't a big deal, then why did her heart hurt every time she thought about it for more than a minute?

What do you think?

Can you relate to Laura's feelings?

_____

_____

_____

_____

_____

A Woman Who Hurts, A God Who Heals

_____

_____

_____

_____

_____

_____

Do you believe you can know a loving, romantic
dating relationship without sex? Why or why not?

_____

_____

_____

_____

_____

_____

_____

_____

_____

_____

_____

_____

Let's read the Bible . . .

"There's more to sex than mere skin on skin. Sex is as much spiritual mystery as physical fact. As written in Scripture, 'The two become one.' Since we want to become spiritually one with the Master, we must not pursue the kind of sex that avoids commitment and intimacy, leaving us more lonely than ever—the kind of sex that can never 'become one.' There is a sense in which sexual sins are different from all others. In sexual sin we violate the sacredness of our own bodies, these bodies that were made for God-given and God-modeled love."

—1 Corinthians 6:16–18 (The Message)

What do these verses mean for us?

I never understood what was so wrong about sex. Why were religious people always talking about it as something bad? What could be wrong with loving someone? Sure, I needed to take care of sins in my life, but sex seemed lowest on the list, not highest. I felt that sex was all about love, and that was the last thing I wanted to throw away.

Then I realized that the sex I had wasn't about love at all. I can remember looking wide-eyed in disbelief at one of my godly woman friends as she said, "A godly man

A Woman Who Hurts, A God Who Heals

would love you by not pushing the physical aspect of your relationship. He would want to honor and protect you. He would love you enough to wait." It sounded too good to be true, but it did sound *good*. A man who would honor me in such a way sounded like a dream, but I longed for a relationship like that. I later understood that God had created me to desire just that—a pure relationship with a man who would honor me and wait until marriage to have sex.

God wants to protect our hearts. He doesn't limit our sexual possibilities because He wants to deprive us of pleasure. He does it because the wrong kind of sex can hurt us in the worst way. He knows what happens to our hearts when the man who made love to us walks out the door. He knows how broken we feel when we are used for our bodies; He hates it! He loves us and He wants to protect us from these broken hearts.

Purity isn't about some law that keeps us from knowing love. In fact, purity is about saving our hearts, so that we *can* know love—true love, godly love. He is a good God, the Giver of all good gifts, and He has so much more for us.

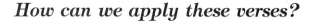

How can we apply these verses?

Would you vow to wait until marriage to have sex? If you are married, will you commit to your husband, knowing that the law of marital faithfulness was put in place to bless and protect you?

If you struggle with saying yes, pen a prayer to Jesus. Ask Him to help you. Sometimes we get so scared of being alone, of letting go, of living a different lifestyle, that we give up and give in. Jesus understands. Ask Him to help you. He will, because He loves you. He knows that it's hard to say no, but He longs to protect you, and He is faithful.

Sometimes we don't know what to pray. God helps us with that as well. The Psalms are a great place to find prayers. David made many mistakes (including falling for another man's wife), yet he was also known as a man after God's own heart. He called out to God no matter the circumstance. Sometimes, when we decide on a different course, we struggle to stay true to that course. Sometimes we don't know how to live a pure life, even if it is the best choice.

A Woman Who Hurts, A God Who Heals

Feel free to make David's prayer yours; I have.

"If you wake me each morning with the sound of your loving voice, I'll go to sleep each night trusting in you. Point out the road I must travel; I'm all ears, all eyes before you. Save me from my enemies, God—you're my only hope!

Teach me how to live to please you, because you're my God. Lead me by your blessed Spirit into cleared and level pastureland." —Psalm 143:8–10 (The Message)

Your love letter . . .

(You can write this one on your own.)

"For I am the Lord, your God, who takes hold of your right hand and says to you, Do not fear; I will help you."

—Isaiah 41:13.

Dearest _____,

_____

_____

_____

_____

_____

_____

_____

_____

_____

_____

_____

_____

Love,

God

More verses. . .

Isaiah 62:3–5

Psalm 27:13–14

Psalm 86:11

Psalm 90:14

1 Thessalonians 4:3–5

Isaiah 43:1

Journal time. . .

Journal at least three days this week. Read the verses listed above, and pick three that you can apply to your life right now. On each day you journal, write the verse you chose and what it means for you. Apply them, and ask for God's help. He'll give you the words.

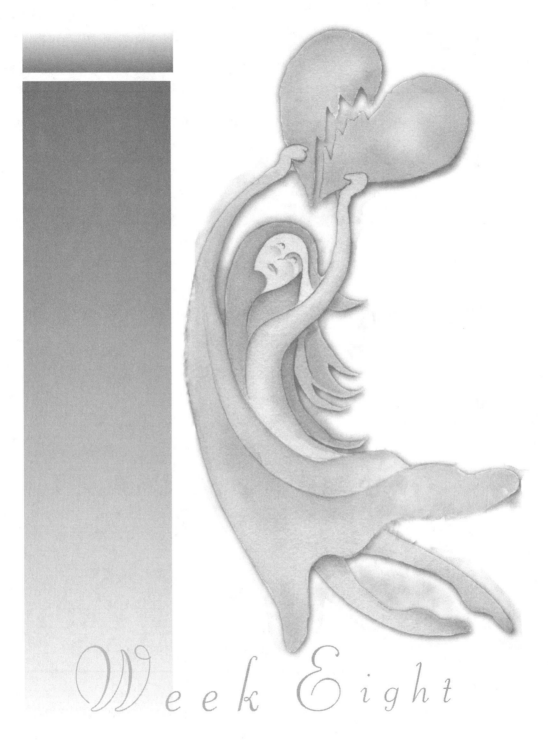

Week Eight

A Woman Who Hurts, A God Who Heals

What's with the Rules?

Patricia couldn't help her feelings. She wanted to do the right thing, get her life together, and be a "good" Christian, but she didn't want to become an uptight, boring stick-in-the-mud. It worried her. What was her life going to become? She didn't know how to ask anyone about it, because thinking such things felt wrong. When she thought about Christians, she thought of grim-faced women with their noses in the air and their smiles plastered on. She thought of somber meetings about spiritual things, meetings that would leave her feeling guilty and somehow "not enough." She thought of all the things she would have to give up—all the things that, on some days, were a lot of fun. She couldn't imagine that life as a good Christian would be very appealing.

Oh, Patricia knew one or two Christians who seemed happy. They were kind and full of laughter and had the spark that she longed for, but that type of Christian was rare. Patricia had the weird sense that she would end up among the ranks of the bored and holy. The picture didn't do much for her.

She sighed. There were too many rules, too many things she couldn't do. Life without all the entertainment she had known would be absolutely no fun. Patricia still wanted to have fun; she couldn't help it.

Eventually, Patricia resigned herself to the whole process. She figured she "ought to," but she wasn't looking forward to it—not at all.

What do you think?

Have you ever looked at Christians the way Patricia did? Describe your picture of a "good Christian."

_____

_____

_____

_____

_____

_____

_____

_____

Do you know any Christians you admire? Do you know any who have that special spark of joy? Write their names and a little about them.

_____

_____

_____

_____

_____

_____

_____

_____

_____

_____

_____

_____

_____

_____

_____

_____

Let's read the Bible . . .

"Since we're free in the freedom of God, can we do anything that comes to mind? Hardly. You know well enough from your own experience that there are some acts of so-called freedom that destroy freedom. Offer yourselves to sin, for instance, and it's your last free act. But offer yourselves to the ways of God and the freedom never quits. All your lives you've let sin tell you what to do. But thank God you've started listening to a new master, one whose commands set you free to live openly in his freedom!" —Romans 6:15–18 (The Message)

What do these verses mean for us?

Freedom! It seems like the ultimate paradox, but living by the guidelines of Jesus offers us freedom. When we live on our own, going after our own pleasure, we end up broken. For example, I never thought I could live without smoking. I didn't want to quit and didn't think I could. It started as something fun, something to do. It became something that controlled me. My lungs were turning black, I couldn't breathe walking up a set of stairs, and I smelled like an ashtray, but I still held on with a vise-like grip.

A Woman Who Hurts, A God Who Heals

Where is the fun in that? I'm a nonsmoker now, and I love it. I love the smells outside; I love to catch a whiff of my fabric softener instead of stale smoke. I love making it up the stairs without hacking out a lung.

Another example: Let's look at the issue of sex. I couldn't imagine staying pure. I was divorced, but I didn't want to be deprived of that intimacy; I wasn't a child. Yet giving myself away left me dependent on guys who couldn't give me what I needed most. I felt alone and anxious and afraid. Where is the fun in that? I can't begin to tell you the things God has done in my heart since I decided to stay pure! He has taught me so much. It's hard to explain the joy in knowing that I will never again be dependent on a man to make me feel valuable or beautiful or special! God has taken that place in my heart. Now, if I choose to love someone, it will be from a place of comfort and security. I never would have imagined that for me! That's freedom!

When we give up our wrong choices, God breaks the chains that we might not realize are there. Satan would love for us to believe that Christianity is boring, that we won't have any fun. What a joke!

Remember that Satan comes to rob us of all that is good. Jesus came so that we would have abundant life. Abundant! That means we live with the knowledge that in Christ we have everything we need—everything we really need. Do you have abundant life? Do you have joy that pierces through the darkest moments and gives you hope? Jesus offers that with His truth.

How can we apply these verses?

I believe that as God brings us close to His heart, we will begin to see the truth about the things He asks us to leave behind. Is God nudging you to walk away from certain things in your life? Would you ask Jesus for help? You can ask Him to help you see the truth; you can ask Him for a taste of His joy and a glimpse of how His way of life gives us freedom.

Share with your Lord the thoughts of your heart.

I also want to encourage you to hang out with the person you listed above, the joyful Christian. Get to know her, build a friendship, and find out more about her freedom. If you couldn't think of anyone,

A Woman Who Hurts, A God Who Heals

get yourself to a local church, and keep your eyes peeled. You'll see them. Take a risk, and get to know them. It will be well worth it.

Your love letter . . .

Combine these three verses:

"To the Jews who had believed him, Jesus said, 'If you hold to my teaching, you are really my disciples. Then you will know the truth, and the truth will set you free.'" John 8:31–32

"There is a way that seems right to a man, but in the end it leads to death." Proverbs 14:12

"'The thief comes only to steal and kill and destroy; I have come that they may have life, and have it to the full.'" John 10:10

Dear _____,

_____

_____

_____

_____

_____

_____

_____

_____

_____

_____

_____

_____

_____

I love you!

   God

More verses . . .

about the freedom that's yours!

Matthew 11:28–30

Romans 8:13–16

Romans 6

Psalm 37:3–6

Psalm 119:44–47

Journal time . . .

Search through these verses, and apply them to what's happening to you today. God is a God of the here and now. He wants to lead you to freedom! Journal at least three days this week.

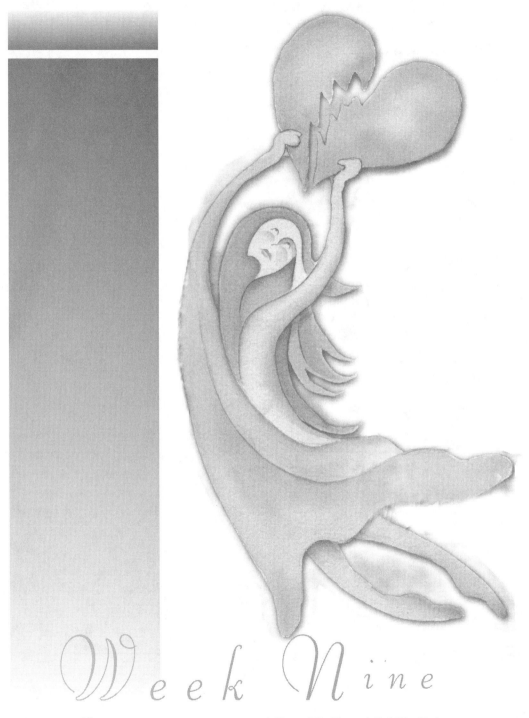

Week Nine

A Woman Who Hurts, A God Who Heals

When Nothing Works

Cara felt as if she was hanging over a deep chasm on one of those ancient rope bridges. Behind her, calling her, was the life she had always known. In front of her was the life she hoped for but hadn't really experienced. She didn't feel as if she could go back to her sin-filled life, and she didn't really want to. Yet when things went wrong, when stress came her way, that was the first thing she thought of. She needed the life that others kept telling her about— a life of joy and freedom, a life where she wouldn't long for the things that hurt her in the end.

She stood between those two lives. Most days she didn't feel strong enough to move forward, and most evenings she sneaked a longing glance back at the old comforts. Some mornings she felt strong, ready to face the day. In the evenings, after a quick look at how many times she had made the wrong choice, everything seemed pretty bleak. Her one Christian friend called it the "place between death and life." "Cara," she had said, "don't give up. This is the hardest part—when you haven't tasted the real joy that comes from freedom and yet you don't have all the things that numbed the pain." To Cara, this made perfect sense. She grieved letting go, realizing that all the things she depended on would never make her life okay. Running to Jesus was her only option, but she didn't feel as if she knew how to do that.

Yet Cara couldn't stop and didn't want to. Something drove her forward. She wanted freedom and joy; she wanted to know Jesus for who He really was. He was calling to her, urging her forward, and waiting on the other side of the bridge.

If she could make it one more step, for today, that would be enough.

What do you think?

Have you ever felt as Cara did—somewhere between the life you knew and the life you've been promised? Write what you have experienced in this process of moving from death to life.

_____

_____

_____

_____

_____

_____

_____

_____

_____

_____

Do your past addictions and longings still have a hold on you? Describe the issues, thoughts, or relationships that have been hardest to walk away from.

_____

_____

_____

_____

_____

_____

_____

_____

The Bible describes the journey of moving from death to life. We are all on this journey together. When we begin to experience a relationship with the One who loves us, we will continue to draw closer. But I believe the process is hardest at the beginning. Sometimes we get stuck on that bridge, and it's hard to move forward. We may try and fail, or we may move back and forth and feel guilty for our weakness. Let's see what Scripture has to say about this path.

Let's read the Bible . . .

"Being confident of this, that he who began a good work in you will carry it on to completion until the day of Christ Jesus." —Philippians 1:6

What does this verse mean for us?

Good news! It means that God is faithful. He understands what life is like on the bridge, and He isn't going to give up on us. It also means that this process is for everyone. Romans 3:23 says, "For all have sinned and fall short of the glory of God." Paul, one of the spiritual giants of the Bible, said it this way in Romans 7:19: "For what I do is not the good

A Woman Who Hurts, A God Who Heals

I want to do; no, the evil I do not want to do—this I keep on doing."

We're not alone. Each of us fights old battles, but Jesus understands. He is gracious. He doesn't give up on us. That doesn't mean we should stay in the middle of the bridge and keep going back and forth. It means that He understands when we fall, and He's not going to let us go. That is the most beautiful thing in the world. I am still amazed by it. I used to wake up certain that God wanted nothing more to do with me, but He never gave up on me. He kept bringing people into my life who loved Him and loved me. He didn't let me go. He wanted me to know the joy on the other end of that bridge!

If you have invited Jesus into your heart, you are His. He will walk with you and love you all the days of your life. He will help you to follow Him, and He will give you bigger tastes of His peace and joy as you pursue Him.

We need to chase God with everything in us. We need to open ourselves up to Him. We need to accept His grace, instead of beating ourselves up, and take another step on the bridge. Once we start tasting the joy and the freedom, we will never turn back. It really is that good.

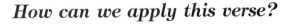

How can we apply this verse?

Do you want the freedom, peace, and joy that Christ offers? Where on the bridge do you find yourself? Have you taken a step toward Christ lately? Would you like to move closer? Write a prayer, expressing your desires to the One who loves you most and who will extend His hand to help you.

Your love letter . . .

> "Forget the former things; do not dwell on the past. See, I am doing a new thing! Now it springs up; do you not perceive it? I am making a way in the desert and streams in the wasteland" —(Isaiah 43:18–19).

These verses have some symbolism in them, but I know you can handle it! Ask God to help you understand what He is saying in these verses. Feel free to apply them to something happening in your life. These words are for you, dear friend! Grasp them as yours.

Dear _____,

_____

_____

_____

_____

_____

_____

_____

_____

_____

_____

_____

_____

_____

_____

_____

_____

_____

I love you!

God

More verses . . .

Psalm 103:1–5

Isaiah 30:18

Romans 8:1

Romans 8:26

Psalm 139:7–8

Philippians 1:9–11

Journal time . . .

Journal at least three days this week. Read the verses listed above, and pick three that you can apply to your life right now. On each day you journal, write the verse you chose and what it means for you. Making these promises yours is an important part of the process!

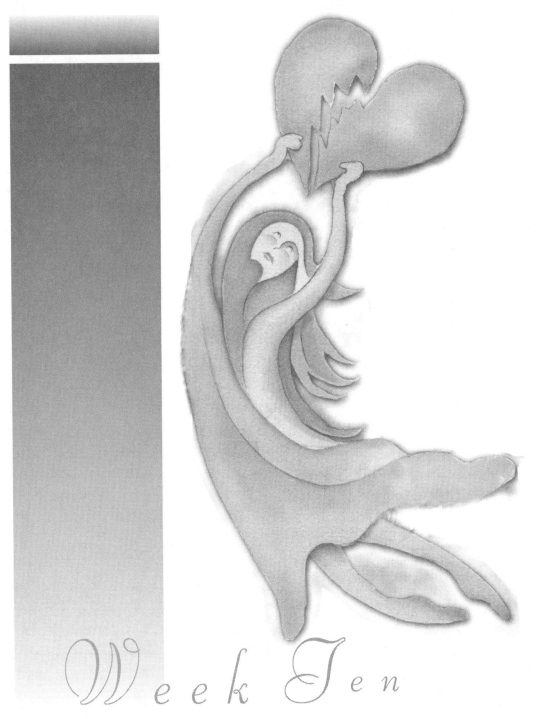

Week Ten

A Woman Who Hurts, A God Who Heals

Girlfriends

Carol rested her head on her shoulder. She was sitting on the couch, her legs curled up, her arms wrapped around her knees. She wanted nothing more than to bury herself beneath the cushions and take a long, uninterrupted break from life. Everything seemed to be coming down around her, and she didn't know what to do. Her first instinct was to grab a big piece of chocolate cake from the refrigerator, but she knew that would only make her more depressed. She thought about trying to pray, but she didn't have the words. She thought about a cigarette but didn't want to start that habit again. So she just sat and wondered about the pain of it all.

The knock on the door surprised her. Carol hadn't invited anyone over, and the last thing she wanted was to chase away a salesperson. She tried to ignore it, but the pounding continued. Her temper flared, and she jerked open the door, ready to unleash her day on whoever dared to interrupt her pity party.

It was Tina! Carol smiled with surprise at her new friend. They'd met only a couple of months before and found that they had a lot in common. Tina was a little stronger in her faith than Carol, but they'd both been through the same type of pain. The connection had been immediate. "What are you doing here?" Carol asked, her pleasure genuine.

"You sounded a little sad on the phone yesterday." Tina paused. "I figured if you were anything like me, you wouldn't call and ask for help. So I'm here to help whether you like it or not."

The tears came immediately. Carol couldn't help it. "You came to help me?"

Tina walked in and shut the door. Without a word, she took Carol into her arms and hugged her close. "Yeah," she said, "I don't know what I can do, but I'd be glad to listen."

Two hours later, Carol closed the door as her friend walked away. She felt better. In fact, she almost felt like a different person! Tina had listened to her and then prayed for her. No one had ever prayed for Carol like that! It made a world of difference. It was as though, since Carol didn't know how to go to God, Tina had gone before her and showed her the way. Carol had never known friendship like that, and she knew she never wanted to live without it again.

What do you think?

Do you have a friend who loves you with God-sized love, who points you to the Father's heart? If you do, thank God for her.

_____

_____

_____

_____

_____

If you don't, do you know of anyone who potentially could be that kind of friend? Write her name.

_____

_____

_____

_____

_____

_____

Let's read the Bible . . .

Naomi was a woman of God. Her husband moved her to a foreign land full of people who worshipped other gods. They had two sons. The sons grew up and married foreign women. Within a short period of time, Naomi's husband and two sons died. Naomi wanted to go back home to the land of her people and her God. Ruth, her daughter-in-law, wanted to go with her. They must have built an incredible friendship, because Ruth was willing to leave everything to stay with Naomi. When Naomi tried to discourage Ruth from leaving her homeland, Ruth said these words:

"Don't urge me to leave you or to turn back from you. Where you go I will go, and where you stay I will stay. Your people will be my people and your God my God" (Ruth 1:16).

What does this verse mean for us?

This story in Scripture says a lot to us about friendship. Godly friendships change lives. Because of Naomi, Ruth could leave her false gods and hopeless future. Because of the love they shared, they

A Woman Who Hurts, A God Who Heals

could encourage each other. Naomi helped Ruth to fall in love with God, and Ruth kept Naomi company on the long journey. Alone, their lives would have turned out much differently. Proverbs 17:17 says, "A friend loves at all times." Ruth and Naomi loved each other through hardship. I don't know about you, but I need that kind of friendship in my life.

I used to be a lone ranger. I didn't mind helping others, but I didn't let people see me sad. I didn't like to need anybody. It felt too uncomfortable, as if they could hurt me more if I needed them. True, they could hurt me, but they could also add to my life. So needing others is risky but worth it.

I can't say when I "got it," when I finally understood how precious friendship is. I just know that my friendships have changed me. Hanging out with godly people helps us in our pursuit of God. I have a friend who loves God no matter what pain she deals with, no matter what circumstance comes into her life. God and she are close! I see the way He comforts her, takes care of her family, and honors her devotion. It makes me want what she has. As Ruth put it, "Your God will be my God" (Ruth 1:16). Friendship with a godly woman gives us an inside

look at how to have a real relationship with our Lord. We need that!

How can we apply this verse?

We may have friendships in our lives with people who don't believe in God. I'm not saying that we should abandon those friendships, not at all! We simply need to add into our lives friendships with people we respect and admire because of their faith. They don't have to be perfect; they just need to love God and be genuine in their hearts.

Building these friendships takes time, but we can start small. Invite someone over for coffee, grab a doughnut somewhere, or hang out on the back stoop at a barbecue. Get to know each other, and see if you find a connection. Pray about it. Ask God to bring someone into your life. Write your prayer; let it come from your heart.

_____

_____

_____

_____

_____

A Woman Who Hurts, A God Who Heals

_____

_____

_____

_____

_____

_____

Now keep your eyes and ears open. God answers prayer. When someone comes to mind or crosses your path, risk reaching out to them. List some possible things you can do together. Then you will feel prepared to ask when the time comes. I'll help you get started on your list:

Go for a walk.

_____

_____

_____

_____

_____

_____

_____

_____

_____

Your love letter . . .

The following verse reminds us that friendship (including friendship with God) will make the difference as we go through life:

> "Two are better than one, because they have a good return for their work: If one falls down, his friend can help him up. But pity the man who falls and has no one to help him up! . . . Though one may be overpowered, two can defend themselves. A cord of three strands is not quickly broken."
> —Ecclesiastes 4:9–10,12

Dear _____,

Remember, My love, you were not meant to do this all alone. Two people working together are stronger than one person working alone.

_____

_____

_____

_____

When you find a friend who loves Me too, we will become as strong as three strands tightly wound together. Nothing will be able to separate us!

_____

_____

_____

    I love you!

    God

More verses . . .

Proverbs 13:20

Hebrews 3:13

Proverbs 27:6

Psalm 68:6

Proverbs 17:17

Journal time . . .

Take some time to write about your current friendships. Consider what you would like to see happen in those (and in any new friendships) over the next few months. Journal at least three days this week. Read the verses listed above, and pick three that you can apply to your life right now. On each day you journal, write the verse you chose and what it means for you.

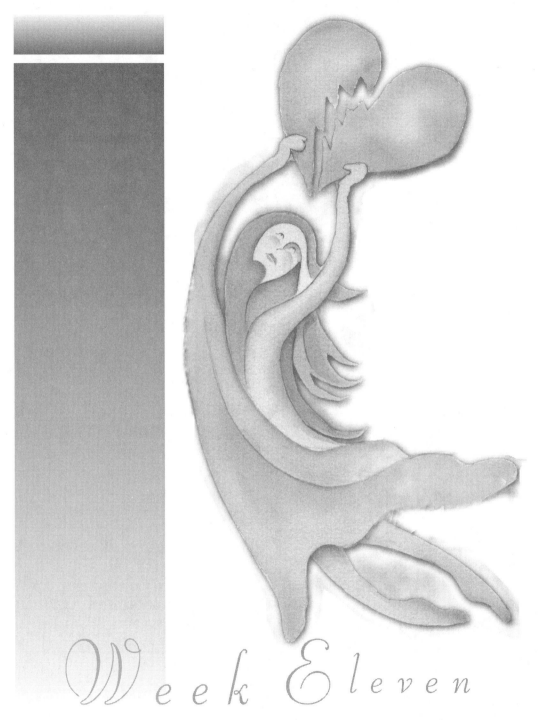

Week Eleven

A Woman Who Hurts, A God Who Heals

Calling His Name

Joanna was at the end of her rope. She had tried everything to make it better, and nothing worked. For twelve years she had been ill, bleeding constantly. The doctors tried different things and finally gave up. All of her money was gone, and her hope was soon to follow. Then she heard about Jesus. People said He was different—that He was kind and cared about the ill, the broken, and the discarded. Joanna knew the feeling of being discarded. According to the law, every day of the last twelve years, she had been "unclean." Not many friends had stayed with her through her illness and shame.

About mid-morning, she heard that Jesus would pass through town any moment. Rumor had it that He was on His way to help the daughter of a synagogue ruler. Oh, she thought, maybe if I can get close enough to touch His robe, I will be healed. That way, He can continue on His journey, and I will be well. She ran quickly through the streets until she came upon the crowd. She pushed through, her heart pounding. She could see Him ahead. Hope flooded her being. Just a little farther, she thought, and I will be able to touch His cloak.

Her fingers reached for the frayed edge, barely brushing it. Instantly, her body was healed. Joanna stopped, overwhelmed by the joy and sense of wholeness that filled her. In her amazement, she didn't realize at first that everyone else had stopped, too. Jesus scanned the crowd. "Who touched my cloak?" He asked. The disciples looked at Him, confused. "This is a big crowd; anyone could have touched your cloak." But Joanna knew what He was talking about, and she came forward, trembling. He stopped the entire procession, and He listened to her story. He smiled tenderly as she shared her hope that if she just touched His cloak, she would be healed.

He placed His hand on her cheek, His eyes full of compassion. To Him, she was anything but "unclean." "Daughter, your faith has healed you. Go in peace and be freed from your suffering" (Mark 5:34).

You can find this story in Matthew 9:18–22, Mark 5:21–34, and Luke 8:40–48.

What do you think?

If you were in that crowd and thought, *If only I could touch His cloak, I would be healed,* what would you want healing for? What hurt, pain, illness, or addiction would cause you to reach to Jesus for healing, hoping that just a touch would make it better?

_____

_____

_____

_____

_____

_____

_____

_____

_____

_____

_____

Jesus stopped the crowd and talked to the woman who reached for Him. He could have kept going. He could have ignored her. She was, after all, healed. He didn't need to speak with her. I believe that Jesus stopped because He wanted her to know that she mattered to Him. He wanted to give her physical healing, but He also wanted to touch her heart. She reached for Him in her greatest need, and He was there. She didn't have to say a word; she just reached out, and Jesus stopped everything to heal her and to love her.

He will do the same for you if you reach out to Him.

Let's read the Bible . . .

"You are kind and forgiving, O Lord, abounding in love to all who call to you. Hear my prayer, O Lord; listen to my cry for mercy. In the day of my trouble I will call to you, for you will answer me." —Psalm 86:5–7

What do these verses mean for us?

God hears our cry and knows our heart. We don't have to come up with some fancy prayers or clean

A Woman Who Hurts, A God Who Heals

ourselves first. The woman who was hemorrhaging reached out her hand, and Jesus was there. David, in Psalm 86, called out, and God was there. We can share whatever is on our heart. Even if we doubt or don't understand, we can talk to God about it.

In Mark 9:14–27, a father comes to Jesus with his son. He says, "If you can do anything, take pity on us and help us." Jesus replies, "If you can? . . . Everything is possible for him who believes." The father struggles with doubt, but instead of pretending to have it all together, he asks for help. He says, "I do believe; help me overcome my unbelief!"

We can go to God with everything and anything. When we call to Him, He hears and He cares. This was a huge discovery for me. I was sad about something, and my first instinct was to find comfort in my old habits. Instead, I tried something different. "Lord," I said, "I'm sad! I don't know what to do, and I want to run away from You. But I won't. I'm standing here and I'm sad and I need You." As I continued to talk about my feelings, peace settled over me. He was there.

We need to pray, dear friend. We need to call to God in every situation. He is waiting to receive us and ready to heal us. He loves to comfort us; this is who He is.

How can we apply these verses?

Something is probably on your mind. You may hurt or have something you can't let go of. You may not feel well, or you may feel great. Use the space below to share with the One who loves you. Your prayer doesn't have to sound fancy, be spelled correctly, or even make sense. Just reach out. He is waiting to stop the procession and talk with you.

_____

_____

_____

Your love letter . . .

"Yet the Lord longs to be gracious to you; he rises to show you compassion. For the Lord is a God of justice. Blessed are all who wait for him!"
—Isaiah 30:18–19

How gracious He will be when you cry for help! As soon as He hears, He will answer you.

Dearest _____,

Oh, how I love you!

_____

_____

_____

_____

_____

_____

_____

_____

_____

_____

With love,

God

More verses . . .

Psalm 40:1–3

1 Peter 5:7

Isaiah 38:5

Joel 2:32

Jeremiah 33:3

Psalm 145:8–9

Journal time . . .

This week, try journaling your thoughts as prayers. You don't have to sound spiritual or avoid writing what's really going on. He's God; He's seen it all. Just write your heart, and let Him be there for you. Don't forget the verses. Pick three, journal your thoughts about one each day, and let them be promises to you!

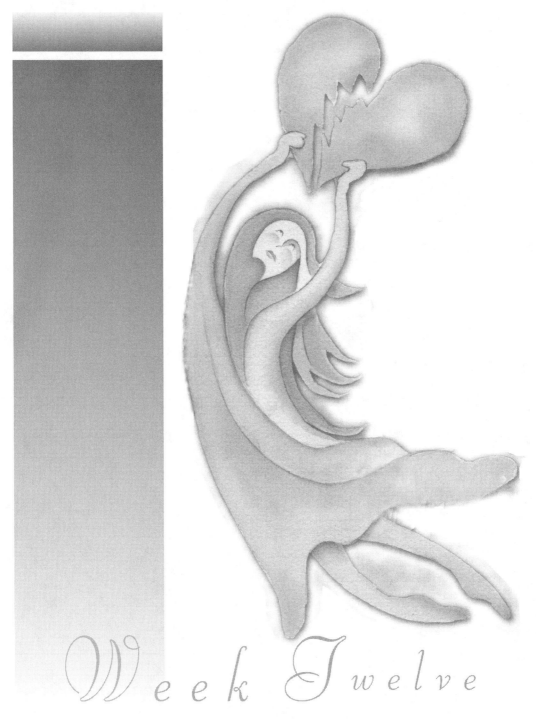

Week Twelve

A Woman Who Hurts, A God Who Heals

Reading His Story

For a long time Sherry thought she knew God. She'd heard about Him in different places, read different things, and formed ideas over time. She never questioned her perception of Him. Didn't everyone have his or her picture of who God is?

Julie helped her see things differently. "Everything you need to know is right here." She tapped her worn Bible. "After I read these words, I started seeing a God completely different from the one I had dreamed up. The God in my head was mean and unforgiving. He was looking for a reason to toss me aside. The God I know from the Bible, the real God, is love. He doesn't just love people, Sherry; He is love. He does everything He can to help us, and He is full of kindness." Julie paused. "And yes, He's holy and perfect. Sometimes He got pretty angry in the Bible, but Jesus shows us His grace perfectly and it's just. . . ." Julie was stumbling over her words in her excitement. "I guess I'm trying to tell you not to trust what everybody else says.

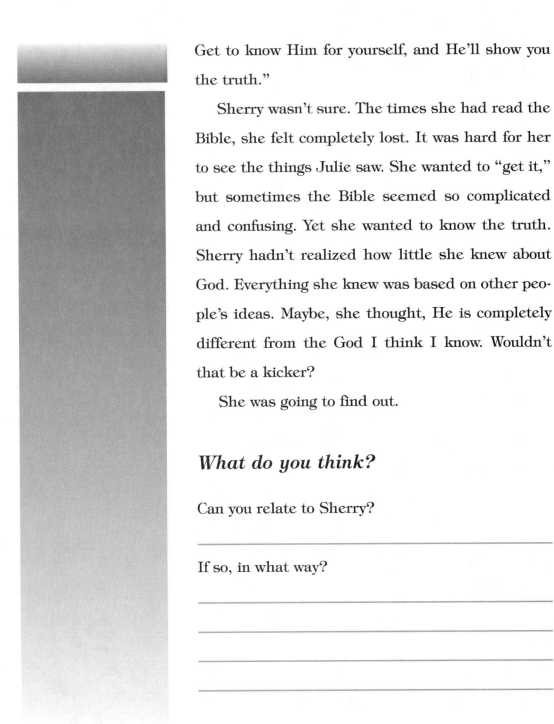

Get to know Him for yourself, and He'll show you the truth."

Sherry wasn't sure. The times she had read the Bible, she felt completely lost. It was hard for her to see the things Julie saw. She wanted to "get it," but sometimes the Bible seemed so complicated and confusing. Yet she wanted to know the truth. Sherry hadn't realized how little she knew about God. Everything she knew was based on other people's ideas. Maybe, she thought, *He is completely different from the God I think I know. Wouldn't that be a kicker?*

She was going to find out.

What do you think?

Can you relate to Sherry?

_____

If so, in what way?

_____

_____

_____

_____

A Woman Who Hurts, A God Who Heals

Where did you learn about God? From your parents?
Friends? TV?

_____

_____

_____

_____

_____

_____

_____

_____

What do you think God is like?

_____

_____

_____

_____

_____

_____

Let's read the Bible . . .

"Ask and it will be given to you; seek and you will find; knock and the door will be opened to you. For everyone who asks receives; he who seeks finds; and to him who knocks, the door will be opened."

—Matthew 7:7

What do these verses mean for us?

God wants to be found. He wants us to know what He's really like. So many sources have Him all wrong. Notice that Jesus says, "Seek and *you* will find" (emphasis added). He doesn't say, "Ask so-and-so, and he'll tell you." He doesn't say that we will automatically know all about Him the minute we open our eyes at birth. He says that we need to seek Him, ask Him, and be ready to hear what He has to say, because it may be different from what we thought!

I used to see God as loving but not loving toward me. Every day I met people who I knew God loved, but I thought He had not stuck with me. I'd disappointed myself and everyone else too many times to be counted as His. I figured He was angry and vengeful, shaking His head as He watched me fall again. Yet as I got to know Him better, I found out that wasn't true!

A Woman Who Hurts, A God Who Heals

How do we find out who God is? We seek Him. The best way to seek Him is to look through His word. Some Bibles arrange Scripture into 365 daily readings. That's a great way to read the Bible in one year. As you read each Scripture, ask yourself two questions: What does this verse say about God? and What does this verse mean for me? A dear friend taught me this method, and I've used it ever since.

Isaiah 55:11 says, "So is my word that goes out from my mouth: It will not return to me empty, but will accomplish what I desire and achieve the purpose for which I sent it." In other words, when we read the Bible, even if we don't understand some of what we're reading, God will work the truth into our hearts. It's like taking a vitamin first thing in the morning. We aren't sure how it breaks down in our bodies, but we know that it makes a difference.

Getting to know God for yourself makes your relationship with Him real. He wants to be found by you. Jeremiah 29:13 says, "You will seek me and find me when you seek me with all your heart." Open the door, ask Him for help, and seek Him. He will be there.

How can we apply these verses?

A great way to start is by asking God to show us who He is. Use the space below to write a prayer. Remember, "'Ask and it will be given to you'" (Matthew 7:7). That's a promise we can hold on to!

_____

_____

_____

_____

Let's look at Isaiah 54:10 and practice getting to know God:

> "'Though the mountains be shaken and the
> hills be removed, yet my unfailing love for you
> will not be shaken nor my covenant of peace
> be removed,' says the Lord, who has compas-
> sion on you."

What does this verse say about God?

_____

_____

_____

_____

_____

A Woman Who Hurts, A God Who Heals

What does this verse mean for me?

_____

_____

_____

_____

_____

Your love letter . . .

Combine these two verses:

"If you accept my words and store up my commands within you, turning your ear to wisdom and applying your heart to understanding, and if you call out for insight and cry aloud for understanding, and if you look for it as for silver and search for it as for hidden treasure, then you will understand the fear of the Lord and find the knowledge of God. For the Lord gives wisdom, and from his mouth come knowledge and understanding."
—Proverbs 2:1–6

"If you seek him, he will be found by you."
—1 Chronicles 28:9

Dear _____,

I love you,

God

A Woman Who Hurts, A God Who Heals

More verses . . .

Proverbs 30:5

Psalm 119:103–104

Matthew 6:33

Colossians 3:16

Psalm 119:33–40

Deuteronomy 11:18

Journal time . . .

Journal at least three days this week. Read the verses listed above, and pick three that you can apply to your life right now. In your journal this week, use the two questions we discussed in this chapter, and apply them to the verses you choose. Ask: What does this verse say about God? and What does this verse mean for me? Ask God to reveal Himself to you.

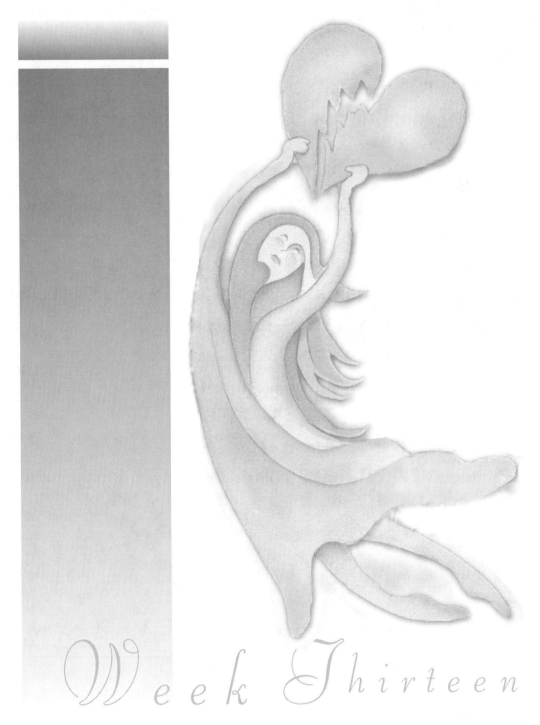

Week Thirteen

A Woman Who Hurts, A God Who Heals

All for Good

Sarah felt their eyes upon her. She could feel their disgust burning into her skin. The Pharisees were known for their religious ways. It was hard for her to feel good about God when so many religious people looked down on her. Then she met Jesus and heard Him teach. He was different in the most amazing ways. He seemed to love people such as her and reach out to the ones everyone else threw away. He found the good when others only saw the bad. Would He find any good in her?

Oh, how her heart longed to make it right. She wanted more than anything to know that all wasn't lost, that she had something to hope for, that maybe with a clean slate she could turn things around. Would this Jesus see her as the sinful woman everyone else saw? Or would He see more? Was there more to see?

Sarah was on her way to find out. She would bring her most precious possession, her jar of alabaster perfume. She would kneel before Him and risk it all to love Him. Maybe He would forgive her. Maybe He would accept her.

Sarah went into the Pharisee's house and looked at no one but Jesus. He noticed her and smiled, welcoming her. Her heart filled with joy, and tears immediately sprang to her eyes. She could feel the stares of the others; she could feel their anger and surprise at her arrival. But she didn't care about them. She cared about Him.

She knelt before Him, her heart bursting with love. No one in all her life had looked at her so tenderly. People laughed or pointed their fingers or looked down their noses at her. But never had anyone touched her heart in a single moment the way Jesus had. She'd done the right thing in loving Him; she knew that now. Her tears spilled over onto His feet, and she mixed the perfume with their dampness. Hope blossomed inside her. This God-man could give her something no one else could. He could wipe the slate clean, wipe away the dirt, and change her life.

You can find this story in Luke 7:36–50.

A Woman Who Hurts, A God Who Heals

What do you think?

Have you ever felt the type of judgment Sarah felt from the Pharisees? Sometimes churches or religious people make the mistake of excluding or judging others. Have you ever felt judged? Describe it.

_____

_____

_____

_____

_____

_____

_____

_____

_____

_____

_____

_____

_____

_____

_____

_____

_____

_____

Let's read the Bible . . .

Judgment such as that makes Jesus angry. Jesus saw the look in the eyes of the Pharisees. This is what He said to them:

> "Do you see this woman? I came into your house. You did not give me any water for my feet, but she wet my feet with her tears and wiped them with her hair. You did not give me a kiss, but this woman, from the time I entered, has not stopped kissing my feet. You did not put oil on my head, but she has poured perfume on my feet. Therefore, I tell you, her many sins have been forgiven—for she loved much. But he who has been forgiven little loves little." —Luke 7:44–47

What do these verses mean for us?

Jesus not only refused to condemn this woman, he also honored her actions. In fact, He knew that because of her past and her brokenness, she would love with more passion than the uptight Pharisees would. He knew that when she gave Him her heart, she would love Him completely.

Can you imagine what that woman's life was like

A Woman Who Hurts, A God Who Heals

after Jesus touched her heart? I imagine she was passionate in her love for Jesus. I have no doubt that when she ran into women from her old crowd, they saw something different in her. She was probably bursting with the good news of Jesus. Can you see her telling, with tears in her eyes, how Jesus touched her heart—how He spoke highly of her in front of those Pharisees? I'm sure her story helped change people's lives!

Romans 8:28 says, "And we know that in all things God works for the good of those who love him." When we risk loving Jesus, as the woman in the story did, He transforms our garbage into gold. I've seen this often in my life, and it amazes me every time. The things I am most ashamed of have helped me relate to other hurting women. People don't see me as far from them; they know I have walked in their shoes. They feel understood.

I never dreamed that I would write about Jesus to anyone. But I am, because He loves me, and He loves you. His love changes us from the inside out.

How can we apply these verses?

Have you risked loving Jesus? Can you imagine all
the broken pieces of your past becoming treasure?
Write a prayer, asking Jesus to help you love Him.
Ask Him to show you a glimpse of the treasure
hidden in your life.

_____

_____

_____

_____

_____

_____

_____

_____

_____

_____

_____

_____

_____

_____

_____

_____

_____

_____

A Woman Who Hurts, A God Who Heals

Your love letter . . .

"The Lord will surely comfort Zion and will look with compassion on all her ruins; he will make her deserts like Eden, her wastelands like the garden of the Lord. Joy and gladness will be found in her, thanksgiving and the sound of singing." —Isaiah 51:3

We can claim as ours the promises God gave to Israel in the Bible. God chose Israel, and when we accept Jesus into our hearts, we become His chosen people. Apply this verse to your situation. For example, "I will comfort you and look with tender sadness on the parts of your body and life damaged by drug use," or, "I will comfort the broken heart that you think will never heal."

Dear _____,

_____

_____

_____

_____

_____

_____

_____

_____

_____

_____

_____

_____

_____

I love you,

God

More verses . . .

Isaiah 55:12–13

Isaiah 54:4–5

Psalm 30:11

Isaiah 61:7

Isaiah 62:3–5

Journal time . . .

As you journal this week, apply the Scriptures carefully to your life. Try to imagine God taking the things you are most ashamed of and making them into your greatest strengths. Write prayers, thoughts, gratitude, or whatever comes to mind. He loves you and wants you to share your heart with Him.

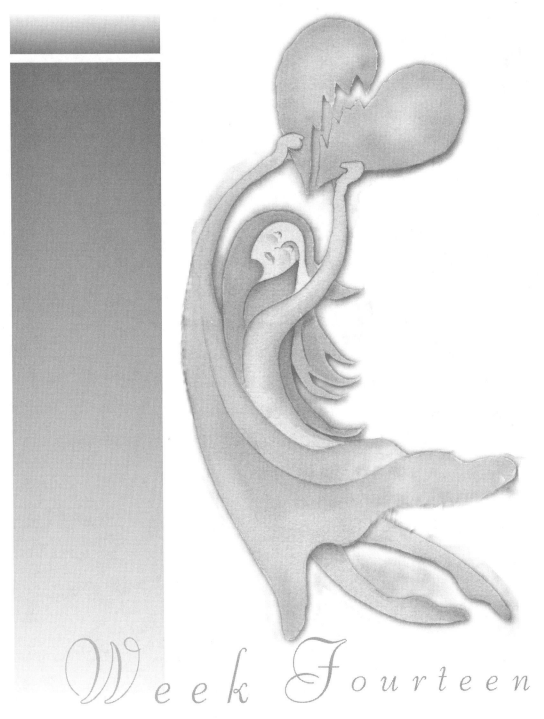

Week Fourteen

A Woman Who Hurts, A God Who Heals

Provider

Ruth wondered how it felt to die. She had enough oil and flour for one more meal. She and her son would eat it together, and that would be it. What would happen after that? She imagined holding her son's thin, frail body as he breathed his last. Though her heart was breaking, no tears came. She was too sad for tears, too broken to grieve.

She heard footsteps and looked up. A man stood there, his head cloaked. He spoke, but it took a moment for Ruth to absorb his words. He asked for a drink. Ruth shuffled for her water jug. "And please," he added, "might I have a piece of bread?"

Ruth looked at him fearfully. She tried to explain that she was gathering wood for her last meal and that she had nothing to give him. "Don't be afraid," said the man. "Make a small cake of bread for me from what you have, bring it to me, and then make something for yourself and your son. For this is what the Lord, the God of Israel, says: 'The jar of flour will not be used up and the jug of oil will not run dry until the day the Lord gives rain on the land.'"

Ruth mixed the last of her oil and flour. She couldn't believe she was making bread for someone else. She looked at where her son lay napping. He seemed so thin, so tired. Was she foolish to trust a feeling—an odd sense that she was supposed to listen and give away the last of their food? What if she was hallucinating because of her hunger? She groaned inside. "O God," she whispered, "let this really be of You."

She finished baking the bread and served it to the prophet of God. With trembling hands she went back to the empty containers. She peered inside the jug and saw something glistening. Half sobbing, half laughing, she dipped her fingers into the oil. The jug had been empty just moments before. She raised her eyes to the heavens. "Thank You, oh, thank You, Lord!"

You can find this story in 1 Kings 17.

A Woman Who Hurts, A God Who Heals

What do you think?

Do you believe that God is capable of providing for your every practical need? Why or why not?

_____

_____

_____

_____

_____

_____

_____

Have you known God's provision? You may have experienced His provision without realizing it was from Him. Reflect for a moment, and describe your experience. (Don't forget to thank Him!)

_____

_____

_____

_____

_____

_____

Let's read the Bible

"And why do you worry about clothes? See how the lilies of the field grow. They do not labor or spin. Yet I tell you that not even Solomon in all his splendor was dressed like one of these. If that is how God clothes the grass of the field, which is here today and tomorrow is thrown into the fire, will he not much more clothe you, O you of little faith? So do not worry, saying, 'What shall we eat?' or 'What shall we drink?' or 'What shall we wear?' For the pagans run after all these things, and your heavenly Father knows that you need them. But seek first his kingdom and his righteousness, and all these things will be given to you as well." —Matthew 6:28–33

What do these verses mean for us?

God loves us down to the details. In the story in 1 Kings and the verses in Matthew, He reminds us what is most important. He says, "Search for Me, do as I ask, and I will take care of the details." He knows we have to pay our rent, feed our children, and make a living. He understands that we have much in life to take care of. But many of us get so caught up in wondering what's going to happen

A Woman Who Hurts, A God Who Heals

tomorrow that we lose sight of what's important today.

God is faithful! He will take care of our practical needs. I can tell you story after story of how God has provided for my daughter and me. We had the anonymous envelope in the mailbox, the article sold at just the right moment, and the friend on my doorstep with an armload of groceries. He knows what we need, and as we learn to trust Him, He shows up in the most creative ways.

Sometimes we hold on to bad things in our lives, because they offer us some kind of security. I know of friends who have stayed in bad relationships because they didn't think they could make it on their own. I know of others who have lived with roommates or stayed in a bad job because they didn't believe God had more for them.

He has so much more. He will not abandon His own! When we boldly pursue God, when we walk firmly where we know He has asked us to walk, He is faithful to take care of our every need. He doesn't say He'll send us on that trip to Aruba or put us up in a condo, but He will always give us what we need most for every day. That is the God we serve.

How can we apply these verses?

Do you trust God with your needs, or do you depend on someone or something else to provide for you? Talk to God, and ask for His help in building your trust and confidence in Him. Write your prayer below.

_____

_____

_____

_____

_____

_____

_____

_____

_____

_____

_____

_____

_____

_____

A Woman Who Hurts, A God Who Heals

As you pursue God and you come across a need in your life, practice bringing it to Him. Often we think of a thousand other places to go before we ask God for help. He is our Father! He longs to help us with everything! Sometimes it's just a matter of asking and then watching for His answer. It may not come in the way we expect it, but His answer will come. He is good, and He loves you.

Your love letter . . .

"Therefore I tell you, do not worry about your life, what you will eat or drink; or about your body, what you will wear. Is not life more important than food, and the body more important than clothes? Look at the birds of the air; they do not sow or reap or store away in barns, and yet your heavenly Father feeds them. Are you not much more valuable than they?" —Matthew 6:25–26

Dearest _____

_____

_____

_____

_____

_____

_____

_____

_____

_____

_____

_____

Love,

God

A Woman Who Hurts, A God Who Heals

More verses . . .

Isaiah 58:11

John 6:35

Philippians 4:19

Isaiah 40:10–11

Psalm 107:8–9

Psalm 40:17

Journal time . . .

Knowing that God is a God of the details, take some time to journal specific prayers this week. Watch how God answers, and make sure you record them when He does. You'll be amazed years down the road when you look back and see how faithful He has been! Journal at least three days this week. Read the verses listed above, and pick three that you can apply to your life right now. On each day you journal, write the verse you chose and specific prayers that come from them. Go for it!

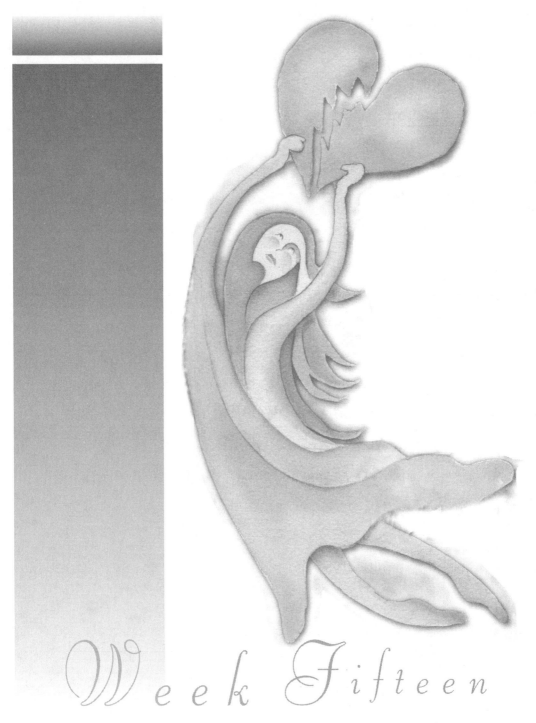

Week Fifteen

A Woman Who Hurts, A God Who Heals

Rest for Your Soul

Kyla took a deep breath and closed the door behind her. She was alone. How long had it been since she had a quiet moment to herself? She glanced heavenward and grinned. "Thank You, Lord" she said.

Kyla had never been to a bed and breakfast. Some friends at church gave her the gift certificate, and now she was here. The evening stretched before her. She had nowhere to be, nothing to do, and only God to connect with. Kyla set her bag at the end of the bed and stretched out on the quilted cover. With her fingers laced behind her head, she closed her eyes and relaxed every muscle in her body. It was going to be a good night.

Five hours later, Kyla felt more at peace than she had in a long time. She'd taken a long walk, soaked in a nice hot bath, and opened her journal. She wrote almost ten pages of thoughts to her Father. She wrote about her frustrations, her joys, and her worries. She felt as though God were really listening, enjoying the time together as much as she was.

She opened her Bible and found a passage in Psalms. She wrote the words in her journal as a note of worship and love.

Never had she felt so connected to God. She didn't feel the same old fears. She knew He wasn't out to get her. He wasn't wagging His finger at everything she did wrong. She was starting to see that He loved her more than anyone else could. He liked spending time with her. He wanted what was best for her. Over time, she had sunk her feet into that love. It felt so natural and real. It was as though her connection to God had finally become a relationship. He was her champion, her safe place, her protector and provider. And she loved Him.

Kyla sat before the fireplace and watched the flames consume the logs. She let herself feel the peace, the quiet in her soul. It was a sweet, tender moment. Spending time with God in such a way felt more pure and perfect than any time she'd spent in the past. She felt no demands, no fear, no desire to be different in order to please. God was filling her, changing her, molding her. She knew instinctively that she would now be able to love others purely. A

A Woman Who Hurts, A God Who Heals

smile danced across her face. It had taken some time alone with God, some time to learn, but she was changing from the inside out. She was grateful.

What do you think?

Can you imagine a relationship with God like Kyla's?

_____

When you imagine spending time with God, what do you feel? Why?

_____

_____

Let's read the Bible . . .

"Morning by morning, O Lord, you hear my voice; morning by morning I lay my requests before you and wait in expectation" (Psalm 5:3).

"Satisfy us in the morning with your unfailing love, that we may sing for joy and be glad all our days" (Psalm 90:14).

"Praise be to the Lord, to God our Savior, who daily bears our burdens" (Psalm 68:19).

What do these verses mean for us?

God longs to bring us to a point where His love is first in our lives. He longs to meet us first thing in the morning, to help us carry our burdens daily, to walk with us through every circumstance. God is not some distant form with no interest in our lives. Matthew 10:30 says that even the hairs on our head are numbered. He knows every detail, every worry, every fear. He knows the pain behind the addictions, the fear behind the anger, the sadness behind the depression. He understands every motive and wants to heal the wounds left behind in our hearts.

The most amazing thing we can invest our time in is a relationship with God. Let Him transform your thinking. Let Him reach in and soften your heart. Let Him draw you close, so that you're dependent only on Him. My heart is full of yearning for you, dear friend! I have walked almost every path in search of something to fulfill me, and nothing exists like the freedom and love I have found in Jesus. Nothing! You will have to work and trust, but I pray that on this day you will decide that He is what you want. We don't need a philosophy or a nicely bound set of rules to break; we need Him. His

A Woman Who Hurts, A God Who Heals

heart, His love, His tenderness, His reality, His purity, His hope, His future.

Read the "Let's read the Bible" verses again. He meets us every morning with His unfailing love. He carries our burdens and hears our cry. Why wouldn't we want to be His? Why wouldn't we do everything we can to draw close to the One who loves us most? Take time with your Savior. He loves you. Keep pursuing Him.

How can we apply these verses?

We have reached the end of our study. This is a critical time. It's so important that you keep working to get to know who God really is. Use the tools you have learned, and walk in relationship with Him. Read His word, spend time with godly friends, call out to Him in prayer, trust His provision, let go of the past, and walk forward with your head high and your heart in His hands.

Write a prayer in the space below. Write what your heart longs for in your relationship to God. Be real; be sincere. He will hear and respond.

_____

_____

_____

_____

_____

_____

_____

As you come to the end of this last chapter, think what you will do. Will you read the Bible daily? Spend time in prayer? Keep searching for more love letters? In the space below, list the tools you plan to use to continue learning about your Savior.

_____

_____

_____

_____

_____

_____

_____

_____

Your love letter . . .

"Take my yoke upon you and learn from me, for I am gentle and humble in heart, and you will find rest for your souls. For my yoke is easy and my burden is light" (Matthew 11:29–30).

"To bestow on them a crown of beauty instead of ashes, the oil of gladness instead of mourning, and a garment of praise instead of a spirit of despair. They will be called oaks of righteousness, a planting of the Lord for the display of his splendor" (Isaiah 61:3).

I know we have discussed this passage in Matthew before, but I think it's a great Scripture to end with. Also let the verse from Isaiah remind you what joy He longs to bring to your heart.

Dear _____,

_____

_____

_____

_____

_____

_____

_____

_____

_____

_____

I love you,

God

A Woman Who Hurts, A God Who Heals

More verses . . .

Isaiah 62:3–5

Isaiah 40:28–31

Isaiah 64:4

Psalm 94:17–19

Psalm 34:8–10

Psalm 30:11–12

Journal Time . . .

Journal at least three days this final week. Read the verses listed above, and pick three that you can apply to your life right now. On each day you journal, write the verse you chose and what it means for you and your future. Ask God to help you understand what He is saying to you. Keep journaling, keep writing, keep applying—for always.